THOMAS HARDY at MAX GATE

THOMAS HARDY *at* MAX GATE

THE LATTER YEARS

DR ANDREW NORMAN

HALSGROVE

First published in Great Britain in 2016

British Library Cataloguing-in-Publication Data
A CIP record for this title is available from the British Library

ISBN 978 0 85704 267 5

HALSGROVE
Halsgrove House,
Ryelands Industrial Estate,
Bagley Road, Wellington, Somerset TA21 9PZ
Tel: 01823 653777   Fax: 01823 216796
email: sales@halsgrove.com

Part of the Halsgrove group of companies
Information on all Halsgrove titles is available at: www.halsgrove.com

Printed and bound in China by Everbest Printing Investment Ltd

CONTENTS

Max Gate, circa 1890s. Photo: The National Trust

ACKNOWLEDGEMENTS

I am grateful to the following: Dr J. H. (Ian) Alexander; Elizabeth Boardman; Vanessa Bourguignon; Jane Bradley; Patricia Burdick; Mandy Caine; Brian Carpenter; Sue Cathcart; Kim Cooper; Caroline Cox; Heather Cowper; Helen Day; Mike Dowell; Dawn Dyer; Aidan Flood; Helen Gibson; Valerie Gill; Jennifer Hancock; Rachel Hancock; John Hayes; Pat Heron; Dr Jonathan Holmes; Vanda Inman; Renée Jackaman; Stephanie Jenkins; Basil Jose and family; Barry King; Joanne Laing; Nuala LaVertue; Mark Lawrence; Andrew Leah; Marilyn Leah; Hannah Lowery; Jasmine Metcalfe; Michael Millgate; Jon Murden; Mike Nixon; Susan Old; Roy Overall; Linda Poulson; Rodney Poulson; Eric H. Prior; Robert Pugh; Stephen Rench; Maureen Reynolds; Michael Richardson; Chris and Sally Searle (The old Rectory, St Juliot, Boscastle, Cornwall); Reg Sheppard; Alan Simpson; Derick Skelly; Alison Spence; Judith Stinton; Lilian Swindall; Reverend Robert S. Thewsey; David Thomas; Deborah Tritton; Toni Tuckwood; Diana and Alan Turner; Jan Turner; Deborah Watson; David Williams; John Williams; Gwen Yarker.

Bodmin Town Museum; Bristol Reference Library; Bristol University Library: Special Collections; University of Bristol; The British Library; Colby Special Collections, Miller Library, Waterville, Maine, USA; Cornish Studies Library; Cornwall County Council; Cornwall Family History Society; Cornwall Record office; Cornwall Studies Library; Dorchester Library; Dorset County Museum; Magdalene College, Cambridge; Oxfordshire Family History Society; Oxfordshire Health Archives; Oxfordshire Photographic Archive; Oxfordshire Record Office; Oxfordshire Studies Library; Oxfordshire Studies: Heritage & Arts; Plymouth Central Library; Plymouth and West Devon Record Office; Poole Central Library; Plymouth Central Library; Queens' College, Cambridge; Redbridge Local Studies and Archives; Royal Geographical Society; Solicitors Regulation Authority; Thomas Hardy Society.

My thanks are also due to the Clarendon Press, Oxford; Cassell and Company Ltd, London; Mid-Northumberland Arts Group and Carcanet New Press; Oxford University Press; Macmillan Publishers Ltd; The Hogarth Press, London; David & Charles Ltd, London; MacGibbon & Kee, London; The Toucan Press, Guernsey; Longman Group Ltd; Colby College Press, Maine, USA.

A special mention is due to the enthusiastic and dedicated staff of the Cornwall Record Office, Devon Record Office, London Borough of Redbridge Local Studies and Archives, and Oxfordshire Health Archives.

I also thank my dear friend of many years, Dr Stuart C. Hannabuss, for his kindly words and valued criticism. And I am especially grateful, as always, to my beloved wife, Rachel, for her invaluable help and encouragement.

FOREWORD

Thomas Hardy was an immensely shy person, who surrounded his house (Max Gate, Dorchester) with a dense curtain of trees; shunned publicity and investigative reporters, and when unwanted visitors arrived unexpectedly, slipped quietly out of the back door of his house in order to avoid them. So that no one should penetrate this mask of shyness, Hardy kept a rigid control over what aspects of his life were to be divulged and what were not. His first wife Emma, behaved in a similar way, at least as far as her and her husband's letters to one another were concerned: she burnt all that she could lay her hands upon.[1] As for Hardy, following Emma's death he burnt, page by page, a book-length manuscript of hers entitled *What I Think of My Husband,* together with most, but not all, of her diaries.[2] When Hardy's second wife Florence, wrote a so-called 'biography' of him, he retained control by dictating to her virtually the whole of the manuscript. When Hardy himself died in 1928, Florence destroyed a great deal more of his and Emma's personal papers.[3] This begs the question, did Hardy have something to hide, a secret of some kind; and if so, is it possible, eight decades after his death, to discover what this secret was?

At first, this appears to be an impossible task, bearing in mind the vast quantity of 'evidence' which was deliberately destroyed by Hardy and his wives, and others,[4] during their lifetimes. Also, when Florence died in 1937, her executor Irene Cooper Willis, destroyed a mass of the first Mrs Hardy's incoming correspondence that had sat undisturbed in her former attic retreat at Max Gate ever since her own death twenty-five years earlier.[5]

However, for the researcher with an open mind, who is alive to the various clues to the many conundrums which Hardy left behind, the task, as will shortly be seen, is not an impossible one.

For much of his adult life, Hardy laboured under a terrible burden of grief, the details of which he kept very much to himself. He required an outlet for this grief; a means of expressing his inner torment, and this outlet came through his writings. Hardy once told his friend Edward Clodd, in respect of his novels, that

> every superstition, custom, &c., described in my novels may be depended on as true records of the same – & not inventions of mine.[6]

Clodd was a banker, popular anthropologist, folklorist, and supporter of Charles Darwin's Theory of Evolution. He had exchanged his original Baptist creed for Congregationalism, then Unitarianism, before finally becoming an agnostic. He lived at Stafford House, Aldeburgh on the Suffolk coast. He and his wife Eliza (née Garman) were separated. (She died in 1911.)

What Hardy did not tell Clodd, and what only a very few of the former's contemporaries managed to discern, was the phenomenal extent to which his own personal life was reflected both in his novels and in his poems. However, even in this he was hamstrung, in that he could not afford to be too explicit – at least while Emma was alive – for fear of offending her.

The purpose of this book is to pierce the veil of secrecy which Hardy deliberately drew over his life; to decipher the coded messages which his writings contain; to find out why his life was so filled with anguish, an anguish which paradoxically led to the creation, by him, of some of the finest novels and poems in the English language. Only then is it possible to discover the real Thomas Hardy!

The journey, which is concerned with Hardy's latter years at Max Gate, Dorchester, is a fascinating one. It leads to many of his former haunts, and to Dorchester County Museum where he spent time, and where many important artefacts associated with him and his life – including the contents of his study – are to be found. It also leads, surprisingly, to various mental hospitals, known in those days as 'lunatic asylums', located in such places as London, Oxford and Cornwall.

ABOUT THE AUTHOR

Andrew Norman was born in Newbury, Berkshire, UK in 1943. Having been educated at Thornhill High School, Gwelo, Southern Rhodesia (now Zimbabwe), Midsomer Norton Grammar School, and St Edmund Hall, Oxford, he qualified in medicine at the Radcliffe Infirmary. He has two children Bridget and Thomas, by his first wife.

From 1972-83, Andrew worked as a general practitioner in Poole, Dorset, before a spinal injury cut short his medical career. He is now an established writer whose published works include biographies of Charles Darwin, Winston Churchill, Thomas Hardy, T. E. Lawrence, Adolf Hitler, Agatha Christie, Enid Blyton, Beatrix Potter, Sir Arthur Conan Doyle, and Robert Mugabe. Andrew married his second wife Rachel, in 2005.

Author's website: www.andrew-norman.com

AUTHOR'S NOTE

My interest in Thomas Hardy was aroused when I discovered a connection between my ancestors and the great Dorsetshire novelist, poet and dramatist: that connection being the Moule family of Fordington.

Fordington, which lies on the outskirts of Dorchester – Dorsetshire's county town – is situated only 2 miles from Thomas Hardy's family home at Higher Bockhampton. My paternal ancestors (who were yeoman farmers) lived here, and were baptized, married and buried at its parish church of St George, by the vicar, the Reverend Henry Moule (1801-1880). The Reverend Moule's son, Horatio Mosley Moule (known as Horace), was Hardy's mentor.

One

THE NATIVE RETURNS

Born on 2 June 1840 in a cottage in the remote hamlet of Higher Bockhampton (which he preferred to call a house) 3 miles from Dorchester, Hardy's accomplishments were already great, despite his relatively young age. At his local school he had gained a working knowledge of Latin, French and German and, encouraged by his mother, was familiar with the great novelists of the day. He had witnessed a public execution; read Charles Darwin's *Origin of Species*, and written what would be the first of many poems viz. *Domicilium*, about his family home. He had lived, for a while, in London where he visited the National Gallery; attended operas and the theatre, and studied to become an architect/surveyor. In 1874 he married Emma Lavinia Gifford, daughter of a solicitor.

Among other places of residence for Hardy were, successively, Weymouth in Dorsetshire; Surbiton in Surrey; Swanage, Sturminster Newton and Wimborne, all in Dorsetshire, and the experience of living in such locations provided him with a backdrop for his novels and short stories. Astonishingly, he had already nine novels to his name, including *Under the Greenwood Tree*, *Far from the Madding Crowd*, *The Hand of Ethelberta*, *The Return of the Native*, *The Trumpet-Major*, and *A Laodicean*.

In June 1883, Thomas Hardy, then aged forty-three, returned to Dorchester (principal town of his native county of Dorsetshire). Here, he and his wife Emma, whom he had married nine years previously, took lodgings in Shire Hall Lane. The following month, accompanied by poet and critic Edmund Gosse, the couple attended a church service at nearby Winterborne Came, conducted by clergyman, poet and Hardy's former teacher, William Barnes. (Barnes had retired from school mastering two decades earlier, in 1864, when he had been offered the living of Winterborne Came-cum-Whitcombe.)

Unable to find a house in Dorchester which suited himself and Emma, Hardy decided to build one, on a plot of land purchased from the estate of the Duchy of Cornwall and situated a mile or so to the east of the town on the road to Wareham.

In this house he would write another five novels; three collections of short stories; eight collections of poetry; an epic drama, and a play in verse. He would travel with Emma to the Continent and to Ireland. He would be accepted by the highest echelons of London society and into their innermost circles, and meet not only the aristocracy, but also the leading literati of the day – for example, poet Robert Browning, and poet and critic, Matthew Arnold.

In July 1910 he would travel to London, to Marlborough House to be invested with the Order of Merit by King Edward VII. Not only that, but the universities of both Oxford and Cambridge would award him an honorary degree of Doctor of Letters.

Sadly however, despite his wonderful achievements in the literary field, all was not well in Hardy's 'Garden of Eden'. His marriage to Emma, whom he had met and fallen madly in love with in March 1870, gradually disintegrated into a meaningless charade, with profound implications both for his social life, writing, and mental well-being.

Max Gate.

Two

MAX GATE: BEGINNINGS

In June/July 1884, Hardy and Emma were to be found in London, meeting artists and writers, including the painters Sir Laurence Alma-Tadema and Edward Burne-Jones.[1] (Since June 1878, Hardy had been a member of London's Savile Club for writers and artists, and since 1879, a member of London's Rabelais (literary) Club, where he met many of the well-known literati of the day.)

On 19 April 1885, Hardy completed the writing of his novel *The Mayor of Casterbridge*. It had taken him at least a year, during which time he had been 'frequently interrupted'.[2] Four decades or so later, he declared that

> the periods of which I wrote in *The Return of the Native*, in *The Trumpet-Major* as well as in *The Mayor of Casterbridge*, are those of my father's time rather than my own. They are, in effect, historical novels.[3]

The novel is set in the eponymous town of Casterbridge (Dorchester) and its principal character is Michael Henchard, a journeyman (hired workman) hay-trusser, who subsequently becomes the town's mayor. That was prior to his decline and fall. *The Mayor of Casterbridge* was published on 10 May 1886 by Smith, Elder & Co.

In London, again in that month of April 1885, the Hardys viewed paintings at the Royal Academy and attended a party given by Lady Carnarvon, wife of the 4th Earl, at which they met Conservative politician Lord Salisbury.

In June, it was time to transfer the furniture from their Dorchester lodging house to the newly completed Max Gate, prior to their taking up residence there on the 29th of that month.

One of the first visitors to Max Gate was Scottish novelist Robert Louis Stevenson and his wife Fanny, in late August 1885. The couple were currently living in Bournemouth in a house called 'Skerryvore'. Subsequent to the visit, the latter described Hardy as

> small, *very* pale, and scholarly looking, and at first sight most painfully shy. His wife... is *very* plain, quite underbred, and most tedious.'[4]

In the drawing room of Max Gate, Hardy would write his next novel, *The Woodlanders*.

The termination of the year 1885 made Hardy 'sadder than many previous New Year's Eves have done'. He asked himself whether the building of Max Gate was 'a wise expenditure of energy', but hinted that there were darker forces at work which had undermined his spirits.[5]

In London once again, in the spring and summer of 1886, Hardy spent time in the British Museum's Reading Room, and attended the House of Commons where the Home Rule Bill for Ireland was being debated. In May he met a 'Hindu Buddhist' who spoke English fluently; was remarkably well educated, and was a 'coach' of the Theosophical Society (which professes that knowledge of God may be gained by intuitive insight into the nature of the divine). Hardy was ever anxious to avail himself of an opportunity to discover the meaning of life. Meanwhile, he went to his Club, observed criminal trials at the law courts and with Emma, attended dinners at various private houses to which they had been invited.

On 7 October 1886, William Barnes died at the age of eighty-five.

It was in the study above the drawing room at Max Gate that Hardy wrote *The Woodlanders*. However, the plot caused him considerable anxiety and he complained of a 'sick headache' and 'a fit of depression' in which he seemed to be 'enveloped in a leaden cloud'.[6]

In *The Woodlanders*, many of Hardy's favourite themes resurface. They include the problems encountered when two persons of different social status fall in love, and when two men compete with one another for the hand of one woman, together with the problems men and women may have of understanding one another. Hardy also stresses that qualities such as loyalty, devotion and steadfastness in a male suitor, ought always to triumph over wealth, property and title.

In the novel's preface, Hardy explains that the book is principally concerned with

> the question of matrimonial divergence, the immortal puzzle [of] how [a couple are] to find a basis for their sexual relation[ship].

This, in turn, begs another question – was Hardy's own sex life with Emma, all that it might be? He also describes how a problem may arise when a person

> feels some second person to be better suited to his or her tastes than the one with whom he has contracted to live.

Hardy had fallen in love with Emma, perhaps at first sight; he had returned from his first meeting with her in Cornwall – 'Lyonnesse' – with 'magic' in his eyes. He had courted her over four and a half long years. And now here, in the Preface to *The Woodlanders*, and only a dozen or so years after his wedding, he appears to be admitting, in so many words, that he regrets the whole affair and wishes that he had married somebody else.

Finally, again in the preface to the novel, Hardy debates the religious aspect of marriage. Is it to be seen as a divinely sanctioned 'covenant' – 'What God hath joined together' – or simply as a secular 'contract' between two people?

On 14 March 1887, Hardy and Emma travelled to London; this time en route to Italy. Here, they visited the cathedrals of Pisa and Milan; the Colosseum in Rome, and the graves of the poets Shelley and Keats – all indicative of Hardy's reverence for both good architecture and poetry. Venice was the city which he appears to have enjoyed the most. In Florence they visited the tomb of poet Elizabeth Browning (wife of poet and playwright Robert), who had died in 1861. They also visited Lucy Baxter, daughter of Hardy's former mentor the late William Barnes, who had settled in Florence after her marriage.

Having returned to London in the spring of 1887, Hardy and Emma trod the well-known path to society gatherings, and again met Robert Browning, now aged seventy-five, with whom they discussed their recent holiday.

Queen Victoria's Golden Jubilee took place on 28 June and they went to view the procession which included vast numbers of royalty.[7] Interestingly, Hardy's *The Trumpet Major,* published seven years previously in 1880, contained an account of King George III's visit to Weymouth. This account had 'interested Queen Victoria' when she read the novel in that same year.[8]

That autumn, Hardy toyed with various ideas for plots for his forthcoming epic drama, *The Dynasts*. Meanwhile, his reading of the poets and the Classics continued unabated.

Towards the end of 1887, Hardy converted the first study into his bedroom, and chose for his second study the smaller bedroom at the rear of the house.

In the spring of 1888, Hardy and Emma again sojourned in London before returning to Paris; this time visiting the Salon, the races at Longchamps, and an exhibition of drawings and paintings by French writer Victor Hugo.[9] On their return, Hardy called upon Lady Portsmouth and, being always one with an eye for a pretty female face or figure, remarked upon how well her ladyship's 'black, brocaded silk' fitted her.[10]

In the late 1880s, Hardy's sisters Mary and Kate Hardy, who had been living at Denchworth in Berkshire, took up residence at No. 12, Wollaston Road, Dorchester: a terraced house which their brother Hardy had purchased for them. They would now commence as teachers at Dorchester's National School. Meanwhile, Hardy's younger brother Henry continued to reside at the Bockhampton family home.

Henry Hardy.
Photo: The National Trust

On 4 May 1888 Hardy's *Wessex Tales* – a collection of short stories – was published by Macmillan. In one of these tales, entitled *The Distracted Preacher*, Hardy made use of anecdotes told to him by his grandfather Thomas I, concerning smuggling on the 'Wessex' coast. ('Wessex', a name that Hardy had borrowed from Anglo-Saxon history for the setting of many of his novels and some of his poems, was used by him to refer to central-southern and south-western England.)

In mid-July at Max Gate, Hardy made a note of some interesting stories that he had heard, for possible inclusion in future novels. Examples included the tale of a man who took 'casts of the heads of executed convicts', and that of a young lady who got married wearing 'a dainty pair of shoes' made for her by a previous suitor, a shoemaker, whose love she had spurned.

In London in Spring/Summer 1889, Hardy was fascinated by painter and master of watercolour, J. M. W. Turner's use of light at an exhibition of his paintings at the Royal Academy. He also compared the techniques of Botticelli and Rubens in their depiction of the 'flesh', vis-à-vis the 'soul'. The fact that both these men were portrayers of the female form, par excellence, would not have been wasted on him! As always, he and Emma attended church services, concerts, plays and, of course, society events.

On 2 July 1889, at a dinner given by Edmund Gosse and his wife Ellen (née Epps), Hardy found himself sitting next to Agatha, whose husband the sculptor Hamo Thornycroft, happened to be in France. He described her as

> the most beautiful woman in England – her on whom I thought when I wrote *Tess of the D'Urbervilles*.[11]

On 23 July 1889, Hardy wrote

> Of the people I have met this summer, the Lady whose mouth recalls more fully than any other beauty's the Elizabethan metaphor 'her lips are roses full of snow' is Mrs Hamo Thornycroft – whom I talked to at Gosses's dinner.[12]

Incidentally, Hamo Thornycroft was the uncle of Siegfried Sassoon.

As for Agatha, she subsequently told her husband that Hardy was 'attentive and nice'. However, said she

> He wanted to persuade me to go with the Gosses to the dinner of the Society of Authors to-night at the Criterion… He considered it was right I shd [sic] be gay while you were away; fearful morals with which to corrupt an inexperienced & innocent person![13]

This statement by Agatha may have been made somewhat jokingly. On the other hand, it may have been a response to a perceived threat to herself of seduction by the flirtatious Hardy.

In late July 1889, at the home of Mary Jeune, Hardy described US novelist Amélie Rives, as

> the pretty woman of the party – a fair, pink, golden-haired creature, but not quite ethereal enough, suggesting a flesh-surface too palpably. A girlish, almost childish laugh, showing beautiful young teeth.[14]

Just as Hardy, in his younger days, had devoted himself to the meticulous study of nature and natural phenomena, so now, amongst the glitterati of London, he devoted himself to the study of the female form with equal diligence and equal satisfaction, no doubt, if not more!

In fact, he had always admired the female form, even when that form was dangling at the end of a rope. This is a reference to Elizabeth Martha Brown who was hanged in Dorchester for murdering her husband: an event, which as a sixteen-year-old, Hardy had witnessed in person. Said he

> I remember what a fine figure she showed against the sky as she hung in the misty rain, & how the tight black silk gown set off her shape as she wheeled half-round & back.[15]

At the end of July 1889 the Hardys returned to Max Gate, where Hardy settled into the daily routine of writing what would be his next novel: *Tess of the D'Urbervilles*. This was not, however, to be a straightforward project. The first two magazines to which he sent the manuscript rejected it on the grounds that it was 'improper', and it was only after he had laboriously edited it, removing parts or all of various chapters, that it was finally accepted for serialization in the weekly newspaper, *The Graphic*.

Hardy, despite the labour of writing, still found the time and energy to record his thoughts and feelings on those subjects which he found intriguing – for example, religion. He had been searching for God for fifty years, he confessed, 'and I think that if he had existed I should have discovered him'.[16] He also found time to write to architect Hugh Thackeray Turner, secretary to the Society for the Protection of Ancient Buildings, objecting to the proposed demolition of the church in the village of Stratton near Dorchester when, in his view, some 'judicious repair' was all that was necessary.[17] At Easter 1890, Hardy visited the grave of William Barnes at Winterborne Came.

In May, when he and Emma were again in London, he sent the manuscript of *A Group of Noble Dames* to *The Graphic*, which agreed to serialize it. This was a collection of short stories – for the background of which Hardy drew heavily on *The History and Antiquities of the County of Dorset* by the Reverend John Hutchins (first published in 1774). For the plots of the stories, however, he relied on

> the lips of aged people in a remote part of the country, where traditions of the local families linger on, & are remembered by the yeomen & peasantry long after they are forgotten by the families concerned.[18]

A year later, *A Group of Noble Dames* was published, in book form, by Osgood, McIlvaine & Co. of London. What did the critics have to say about *A Group of Noble Dames*? In the words of one, it was a

> pageant of disastrous marriages, confessed and unconfessed adulteries, complicated illegitimacies, sudden deaths, suspected crimes [and] bizarre cruelties... among the Wessex gentry of some generations back.[19]

In London again, in 1890, Hardy declared that he was 'getting tired of investigating life at music halls and police courts', which appears to have been his principal preoccupation during that season in London. Nonetheless, at the former events he was much taken with the beautiful actresses and dancers with their 'lustrous eyes and pearly countenances'.[20]

When, in September 1890, Emma's father John Gifford died, Emma left London to attend his funeral in Devonshire. Hardy did not accompany her. Thereafter, Hardy generously arranged an annuity for Emma's niece and nephew; (Ethel) Lilian (Attersoll) Gifford, and her brother Gordon Gifford. That August, Hardy and his brother Henry, visited Paris together.

For Hardy, the irony of the fact that he, an outspoken critic (through his writings) of the upper classes, was now coming into contact more and more not only with the 'cream' of London society, but also with the gentry of Dorsetshire, would not have escaped him. For example, in January 1891 he attended a ball given by Mrs Brinsley Sheridan (a descendant of Irish dramatist Richard Brinsley Sheridan) at her home, Frampton Court, Frampton, near Dorchester. To this, Emma arrived on horseback: horse riding being a favourite pastime of hers.

In the spring of 1891, Hardy was elected to the Athenaeum (a London gentlemen's club), from the balcony of which he saw the German emperor,

Wilhelm II pass by.

Despite his literary success, Hardy was still unable to afford a (second) home in London, and he and Emma were obliged to find rented accommodation for their annual spring sojourns in the capital. At a luncheon at (Susan Elizabeth) Mary Jeune's in July, Hardy mentions sitting between 'a pair of beauties': the one with 'violet eyes' being 'the more seductive'; while the other was 'more vivacious'.[21] Mary, formerly Stanley (née Stewart-Mackenzie), who, in August 1881, married lawyer Francis Jeune, 1st Baron St Helier, was related to Emma Hardy by marriage. The Hardys often stayed with the Jeunes at their London home. Of Hardy, she declared

> I think he is the most modest person I ever came across, and he hated the publicity which necessarily surrounded him, and shrank from it as much as the most timid woman.[22]

In September, Hardy and Emma visited Scotland and many of the places depicted by Sir Walter Scott in his novels.[23] In that year of 1891, Emma's mother died. It is not known if Emma attended the funeral.

When Hardy commenced a new novel he preferred, where possible a), to have a change of location and b), to select a brand new pencil with which to write it. Accordingly, for *Tess of the D'Urbervilles* he moved out of his old study and into a new one, situated at the rear of Max Gate with a window facing west.

The story contains many of Hardy's favourite themes: the class system; falling in love; but crucially, how Church and State combine to condemn and persecute a woman for giving birth out of wedlock to a 'bastard', as such a child was called in those times; also, how women are vilified for indulging in sexual intercourse prior to marriage, but men less so.

Tess of the D'Urbervilles therefore provided Hardy with a vehicle for yet another outburst against the victimisation of the weak and oppressed, perpetrated by the upper classes and a rigid fundamentalist religion, and enforced by a callous and impersonal legal system.

Tess of the D'Urbervilles was published in late November 1891 by Osgood, McIlvaine & Co. It became a talking point throughout the land and was quickly translated into several languages, including Russian. Despite this, many libraries refused to stock it. Its review in *The Quarterly* was to offend Hardy deeply. The article, he said, was smart and amusing, but at the expense of 'veracity and sincerity'. 'If this sort of thing [criticism] continues', he said, there would be 'no more novel-writing for me'.[24]

Journalist Raymond Blathwayt, suggested to Hardy that he might have arranged a happier ending for the eponymous heroine of *Tess of the d'Urbervilles*. To this, Hardy replied

> No, the optimistic 'living happily ever after' always raises in me a greater horror by its ghastly unreality than the honest sadness that comes of a logical and inevitable tragedy.[25]

On 20 July 1892, Hardy's father Thomas II died. His last request had been for a drink of water from the well, which led him, when he had tasted it, to say: 'Now I know I am at home'.[26] He was buried in Stinsford churchyard, and it was Hardy himself who designed his tombstone. Whereupon, Hardy's cousin Mary Elizabeth ('Polly') Antell, daughter of Jemima's sister Mary (who had died in the previous year, 1891), took up residence at the Bockhampton family home as a female companion for the widowed Jemima. From then on, the family business was carried forward by Hardy's brother Henry, who also continued to reside at the family home.

In October, Hardy attended the funeral, at Westminster Abbey, of poet Alfred, Lord Tennyson who had died on the 6th of that month.

In May 1893, Hardy and Emma visited the Vice-Regal Lodge, Dublin, Ireland, at the invitation of Richard Monckton Milnes, Lord Houghton, that country's Lord Lieutenant. His Lordship was a man of letters who had known Hardy since the year 1880, both being members of the Rabelais Club. Lord Houghton's daughter was Florence Henniker, who in the previous year had married Major General Arthur Henniker-Major. She was Hardys junior by fifteen years. On the 24th of that month in Dublin, the Hardys witnessed Queen Victoria's Birthday Review.

Having returned to England, Hardy began a prolific and detailed correspondence with Florence Henniker, confiding in her and being solicitous for her welfare, as if she were an acquaintance of longstanding. He hoped she would always be 'among the most valued of my friends'; he enquired whether she would be at Lady Jeune's dinner on 9 July, and if so, he too would be there, despite having a previous engagement – which he would cancel; he enquired about her recent cold; 'It would delight me much to hear from you', he told her. Clearly, Hardy was totally smitten by her! And when Hardy, together with Emma and Florence Henniker arrived in London for the forthcoming season, he and the latter spent a great deal of time together.

However, matters between Hardy and Florence Henniker came to a head on 8 August 1893, when they met at Eastleigh in Hampshire; she having arrived from London and he from Max Gate. En route to Winchester the pair had lunch at the George Inn in that city, and attended evensong at the Cathedral. But matters evidently did not proceed as Hardy would have wished, and typically, he expressed in poetry the trauma which he experienced as a consequence of this encounter, as if this was for him a), the veritable end of the world, and b), the first time that he had been disappointed in love! In *The Months Calendar*, for example, he wrote

Tear off the calendar
Of this month past,
And all its weeks, that are
Flown, to be cast
To oblivion fast!

Darken that day
On which we met,
With its words of gay
Half-felt regret
That you'll forget!

And the last verse reads

For then it was
You let me see
There was good cause
Why you could not be
Aught ever to me!

According to Hardy enthusiast Hermann Lea,[27] and based presumably on what the latter had told him, Hardy's poem *At an Inn,* refers to the George Inn at Winchester, and it may also, therefore, be taken to relate to Florence Henniker.

When we as strangers sought
  Their catering care,
Veiled smiles bespoke their thought
  Of what we were.
They warmed as they opined
  Us more than friends –
That we had all resigned
  For loves dear end.

The third verse reads:

And we were left alone
  As loves own pair;

Yet never the love-light shone
  Between us there!
But that which chilled the breath
  Of afternoon,
And palsied unto the death
  The pane-fly's tune.

The 'pane-fly's tune' is presumably the agonizing whine that the dying house fly makes when it finds itself trapped indoors by a window pane. And in the final verse, the anguished Hardy writes:

As we seemed we were not
  That day afar,
And now we seem not what
  We aching are.
O severing sea and land,
  O laws of men,
Ere death, once let us stand
  As we stood then!

Any record of what actually transpired between Hardy and Florence Henniker in Winchester was probably lost in the conflagration at Max Gate, during which, after Hardy's death, Florence Hardy burnt a great deal of his correspondence. However, his poems leave little doubt as to the reason for the rift between the two, i.e. Hardy wanted more from Florence than she was prepared to give, and this may well have included sexual intercourse. So why did Florence demur? Possible reasons are her Catholicism and resultant unwillingness to break her marriage vows by committing adultery; a sense of loyalty to her husband Major Henniker; that she had simply never viewed her relationship with Hardy as anything other than platonic.

Hardy was equally downcast when Florence Henniker failed to meet him at an agreed rendezvous at the British Museum. This too, he reflected in a poem, *A Broken Appointment*.

        You did not come,
And marching Time drew on, and wore me numb. -
Yet less for loss of your dear presence there
Than that I thus found lacking in your make
That high compassion which can overbear
Reluctance for pure loving kindness' sake
Grieved I, when as the hope-hour stroked its sum

You did not come.

In the second and final verse, Hardy is not only downcast bur reproachful towards Florence.

You love not me,
And love alone can lend you loyalty;
-I know and knew it. But, unto the store
Of human deeds divine in all but name,
Was it not worth a little hour or more
To add yet this: Once you, a woman, came
To soothe a time-torn man; even though it be
You love not me?

The fact that Hardy's poem *The Division,* bears the date 1893, suggests that it too relates to Florence Henniker.

Rain on the windows, creaking doors,
With blasts that besom the green,
And I am here, and you are there
And a hundred miles between!

O were it but the weather, Dear,
O were it but the miles
That summed up all our severance,
There might be room for smiles.

But that thwart thing betwixt us twain,
Which nothing cleaves or clears,
Is more than distance, Dear, or rain,
And longer than the years!

The strength of Hardy's sentiments thus expressed indicate a), that for him, meetings with Florence Henniker were intended to encompass far more than simply visits to places of interest. In other words, such meetings were intended to be more in the nature of a tryst, and b), that he was a man desperate for romance.

Nevertheless, despite this setback, Hardy wrote to Florence Henniker only nine days later, on 17 August 1893 and declared, 'I am always your friend'.[28] And, subsequently, they struck up a lifelong correspondence.

In that year Hardy's brother Henry, commenced the building of a house

'Talbothays', at West Stafford, situated a mile or so to the east of Max Gate; the architect being none other than his brother Thomas. On completion, Talbothays was let. Meanwhile, Henry continued to reside at the Bockhampton family home.

On Christmas Eve 1893, at Max Gate, Hardy and Emma received carol singers who, together with their lanterns, stood under the trees and sang to the accompaniment of a harmonium.

Three

JUDE THE OBSCURE: ALTERATIONS AND EXTENSIONS TO MAX GATE

In February 1894 a collection of Hardy's short stories was published by Osgood, McIlvaine & Co. under the title *Life's Little Ironies*. The Hardys spent that spring in London in rented accommodation in their customary way, viz. attending dinners, plays and the theatre. They took their servants with them. With the income from Hardy's books, the couple had now come up in the world!

At this time, Hardy was still engaged in his never-ending quest to understand women, and an idea was developing in his mind for a novel in which the problem of male/female relationships would be explored in full.

Four years previously, in 1890, Hardy had 'jotted down' the plot for what was to become *Jude the Obscure*.[1] In 1892, he had visited the village of Great Fawley in Berkshire, from where his maternal grandmother Mary Head (who had experienced a miserable life as an orphan), had originated. The hero of the story Jude Fawley, would derive his name from this village.

In *Jude the Obscure*, the plot develops in Hardy's characteristic style, taking innumerable twists and turns as he introduces not one, but a plethora of proverbial spanners into the works in order to thwart and disrupt the lives of his 'characters'. The novel also reflects Hardy's abhorrence of cruelty to animals, and his reverence for education and learning; also, the seeming contradiction between knowledge and experience on the one hand, and religious 'belief' on the other.

In the novel, the hero Jude's great-aunt, Drusilla, issues a dire warning to him about the consequences of matrimony. Said she

> Jude, my child, don't you ever marry. Tisn't for the Fawleys to take that step any more. The Fawleys were not made for wedlock: it never seemed to sit well upon us. There's sommat in our blood that won't take kindly to the notion of being bound to do what we do readily enough if not bound.

Drusilla subsequently apprises Jude of the various tragedies that have befallen his forebears, including his own parents. Nevertheless, Jude marries Arabella Donn, daughter of a pig breeder.

After Drusilla's death, Jude tells his cousin Sue Bridehead that his great-aunt had once told him that the Fawleys particularly… members of our family… made bad husbands and wives. Certainly we made unhappy ones.

Mrs Edlin, formerly a friend of the late Drusilla, reinforces this idea when she tells Jude and Sue, about certain mishaps which their common ancestors had experienced.

They was always good-hearted people… wouldn't kill a fly if they knowed it, but things happened to thwart 'em.

This leads Sue to say, despairingly

It makes me feel as if a tragic doom overhung our family, as it did the house of Atreus [a tragic family from Greek mythology].

Is it conceivable that Hardy had his own circumstances – i.e. his marriage to Emma in mind when he wrote these words – not that his family and hers were related in any way?

Sue marries schoolmaster Richard Phillotson, but she feels trapped in her marriage, and can see no way out.

Though I like Mr Phillotson as a friend, I don't like him – it is a torture to me – to live with him as a husband!

What is the real significance of *Jude the Obscure*? In the Preface, Hardy explained the reasons why he had written the novel. It was, he said

simply an endeavour to give shape and coherence to a series of seemings [apparent, but perhaps not real, occurrences], or personal impressions.[2]

The implication is, therefore, that yes, Hardy *was* writing about his personal experiences in an effort to make sense of them, and that the narrative of *Jude the Obscure was* a reflection of the author's own troubled marital life.

'The marriage laws', said Hardy in a postscript to *Jude the Obscure*, written sixteen years after its publication in April 1912, were

used in great part as the tragic machinery of the tale [his own opinion being that] a marriage should be dissolvable as soon as it becomes a cruelty to either of the parties – being then essentially and morally no marriage.[3]

When Jude first set eyes on Sue he clearly fell head over heels in love with her, and experienced an 'unmistakeably… sexual' attraction to her. However, he feels that he, in return, has received only a fraction of the love from Sue that he gave to her. Did Hardy feel similarly about Emma? And furthermore, was the writing of the novel, in reality, an attempt on his part to understand the differences between himself and her, in the desperate hope that these differences might be resolved?

Said Sue to Jude

> You forget that I must have loved you, and wanted to be your wife, even if there had been no obstacle [i.e. the fact that Jude was already married, to Arabella Donn].

But, she continued, there was another impediment, in that 'we are cousins, and it is bad for cousins to marry'.[4] This implies that the author Hardy was well aware that, in the case of cousin marriages, there was an increased risk that their offspring might be born with physical or mental defects.[5]

Subsequently, and despite the 'marriage laws', Jude and Arabella divorce, as do Sue and Phillotson. This leaves the pair free to marry. However, one of Sue's reasons for fearing the marriage ceremony, Hardy explained to Edmund Gosse, was that she was afraid that it would be

> breaking faith with Jude to withhold herself [from having sexual intercourse with him] at pleasure, or altogether, after it; though while uncontracted, she feels at liberty to yield herself as seldom as she chooses. This has tended to keep his [Jude's] passion as hot at the end as at the beginning, & helps break his heart. He has never really possessed her as freely as he desired.[6]

Was this an admission by Hardy that he himself, was broken-hearted, after years of sexual frustration as far as Emma was concerned, and perhaps even an indication by him that his marriage to her was never consummated? If so, it is surprising that, despite all, the couple maintained an outward veneer of normality in that Emma continued to travel with Hardy and to attend social functions with him.

In June 1894, in an article published by the *New Review*, Hardy was prompted to ask whether young women should be informed of the facts of life *prior* to marriage, instead of being left to discover them afterwards. The inference here is that had Emma been apprised of precisely what the act of sexual intercourse entailed, she would not have consented to marry Hardy, which would have saved them both much anguish. And Hardy is scarcely able to contain his sense of bitterness and disillusionment when he goes on to enquire whether marriage was 'such a desirable goal for all women as it is assumed to be'. Or was it the truth that that particular institution had 'never succeeded in creating that homely thing, a satisfactory scheme for the conjunction of the sexes'?[7] Again, reading between the lines, this appears to be yet another cry for help from Hardy.

The novel was serialized, commencing in November 1894 in *Harper's Magazine*, but only after certain changes were made at the insistence of the publisher. Hardy then restored the work to its original version – an exhausting process – prior to its publication in book form a year later, in November 1895, by Osgood, McIlvaine & Co.

From the summer of 1894, Emma used the attic at Max Gate as her sleeping quarters and retreat – boudoir – describing it as her

> sweet refuge and solace [where] not a sound scarcely penetrates hither.[8]

Thomas Hardy in the 1890s. Photo: Dorset County Museum

Works written by her in her attic rooms included *Some Recollections* – an account of her childhood, of her romantic meeting and courtship with Hardy, and of her early married life; *Alleys* – a collection of 15 poems on such subjects as nature and patriotism, but mainly on religion; *Spaces* – a work of prose concerned with such subjects as heaven, Satan, the Day of Judgement etc.; some evangelical pamphlets; and *The Maid on the Shore* – a romantic novella inspired by her husband's novel, *A Pair of Blue Eyes*.

Following his success as an author, Hardy, from 1894 to 1895, could afford to make considerable enlargements and adaptations to Max Gate. On the ground floor, both dining room and drawing room were enlarged. At the rear, a kitchen, pantry, larder, scullery, boot and knives room, coal house, apple store, and woodshed were added.

On the first floor, an extra room was added at the rear, beyond which was a smaller room, with its own staircase. As for the attics, a new servant's room was added at the rear, complete with its own staircase. On the south-east corner, a second turret was added to match the pre-existing one opposite, thus giving symmetry to the whole. Finally, a flushing toilet was installed in the apple store for the use of the servants.

Another female beauty with whom Hardy fell in love was Agnes Geraldine, daughter of archaeologist and ethnologist General Henry Augustus Lane Fox Pitt-Rivers of Rushmore in Wiltshire and his wife Alice (sister of Mary Jeune's first husband Constantine Stanley). In July 1882, Agnes had married Walter John Grove (later Baronet). A fledgling journalist, she was a champion of women's suffrage and animal rights, and commentator on social issues.

At Rushmore, the General had created his Larmer Tree pleasure park, including theatre. (This was a reference to a tree which had once marked the boundary between the counties of Wiltshire and Dorset.) On 4 September 1895

> on the occasion of the annual sports at the Larmer Tree, and a full moon and clear sky favouring, the dancing on the green was a great success.

On that occasion it was Hardy

> who started the country dances, his partner being Mrs [Lady] Grove. This was the last occasion on which he [Hardy] ever trod a measure, according to his recollection.[9]

Hardy subsequently told Florence Henniker that his visit to the Pitt-Rivers had been 'the most romantic time I have had since I visited you at Dublin'.[10] From then on, Hardy and Agnes corresponded frequently: he helping her to fulfill her own literary ambitions. Also, they met from time to time at social functions.

Sculptor Hamo Thornycroft and his wife Agatha, visited Max Gate on 21 September 1895 (and several times thereafter). The Thornycrofts, as Hamo noted in his diary, had recently discovered the joy of bicycling and they, in turn, encouraged the Hardys to do likewise. And sure enough, shortly after their visit, Hardy purchased a bicycle for himself and one for Emma. He subsequently became a prodigious cyclist, visiting such places as Bristol, Gloucester, Cheltenham, Sherborne, Poole, and Weymouth – 'sometimes with Mrs Hardy, sometimes with his brother'.[11]

Said Emily Weber

> I can remember... Mrs Hardy in her green velvet dress. This matched her green painted bicycle. She was a keen cyclist and always referred to her cycling machine as 'my little grasshopper'.[12]

12 January 1896, actress Beatrice Campbell (née Tanner) – known as 'Mrs Patrick Campbell' – visited Max Gate, and on 12th of that month declared

> It is lovely down here. This afternoon Mr Hardy has been playing old English dances on his fiddle and I have been dancing (improvised steps!) to them. It was a sight for London Town.[13]

Continued Emily

> On one of our visits to Hardy we took some Spanish friends and they sat on the floor in the drawing room and sang Spanish folk songs with great gusto to the evident pleasure of both Mr Hardy and his wife. Hardy, in conversation with these Spaniards, showed a remarkable knowledge of Spain and its history. Hardy was like that, no matter what the subject, he always knew a great deal about it. His wide general knowledge greatly impressed me.[14]

The peace, however, was not to last, for the 'earthquake' which followed the publication of *Jude the Obscure* was of an even greater magnitude than that which had followed *Tess of the D'Urbervilles*. In that month of January 1896, Hardy complained to Scotsman, critic, and journalist William Archer, that the novel had been misinterpreted, in that the theme of 'the doom of hereditary temperament & unsuitable mating in marriage' had been taken as an attack on that institution in general. He also denied that the book was in any way immoral.[15] The following month he complained to Emma that he had 'fearful depression' and a 'slight headache'.[16]

That section of the press which had greeted *Jude the Obscure* with outrage and disgust now chose to ignore Hardy and his works. As for the Bishop of

Wakefield, he announced that he had thrown the novel into the fire. Hardy reacted to this news by remarking, dryly, that 'theology & burning' had been bed fellows for many centuries, and he supposed that 'they will continue [to be] allies to the end'.[17]

In a postscript to *Jude the Obscure*, written some years later, Hardy made further comments on the novel and on its reception by the public and the critics: an experience which, he declared, had completely cured him of any further interest in novel writing.

In London for the 1896 season, Hardy and Emma met with such people as Susan, Countess of Malmesbury (a writer); the Duchess of Montrose; Theresa, Lady Londonderry, and the author Henry James. August found the couple at Stratford-upon-Avon, where they visited places associated with William Shakespeare.

September found them in France and in Belgium where Emma, who had by now given up horse riding, purchased a bicycle which she imported into England. Meanwhile Hardy, doubtless with *The Dynasts*, which he was about to compose in mind, revisited the site of the Battle of Waterloo. This epic drama was to be based on the real-life mighty struggle between the French army, commanded by Emperor Napoleon Buonaparte, and the British army, commanded by the Duke of Wellington.

In June he wrote from London to his sister Kate, offering to obtain for her 'pianoforte pieces' or 'dance music' from the music publisher, Chappell.[18]

In October 1896, Hardy bewailed the fact that if he were

> to cry out in a passionate poem that the Supreme Mover... [which he believed controlled all earthly happenings, and which he would shortly allude to in *The Dynasts*] must be either limited in power, unknowing, or cruel – which is obvious enough, and has been for centuries... [then this would] set all the literary contortionists jumping upon me, a harmless agnostic, as if I were a clamorous atheist.[19]

Kate Hardy.
Photo: The National Trust

In regard to *Jude the Obscure*, Hardy's wife Emma was also to be numbered amongst his critics for, in the words of her nephew Gordon Gifford, she 'strongly objected to this book and, I think, the outlook of some of the characters depicted therein'.[20] Clearly, she had a), recognized herself in the novel and b), felt that she had been portrayed in a poor light.

Two poems which Hardy had composed in the year 1875, reinforce the notion that there was a longstanding rift between himself and Emma. The lines 'Wasted were two souls in their prime' (from *We Sat at the Window*), and 'Between them lay a sword' (from *To a Sea Cliff*) are particularly significant.

Why, in view of seeming incompatibility of the couple, did Hardy not simply walk away from Emma and petition for a divorce? There were several possible reasons why he rejected this course of action: a), pride – in that he wished to avoid loss of face; b), a desire to avoid a scandal, which may have led to him being ostracized by society and shunned by his publisher; c), a feeling that he was responsible for Emma's welfare; d), a dread of the inevitable upheaval which would ensue, including the disruption of his writing. The over-riding reason, however, may have been that the vision of Emma as he had once perceived her – the beautiful woman who had transfixed him, perhaps at first sight – had not left him, and it never would. And he would spend the remainder of his days in bewilderment, searching for his lost Emma, and hoping against hope that the wondrous vision would return.

Four

HARDY REVEALS HIMSELF THROUGH HIS WRITING

Hardy's novel *The Well-Beloved* (originally entitled *The Pursuit of the Well-Beloved*) was published by Osgood, McIlvaine & Co., in March 1897. However, the bulk of it was written before the publication of *Jude the Obscure*.

This is a novel which embraces the idea that a person may fall in love, and continue to do so throughout his or her life, not with a particular physical being, but with an idealized conception of perfect beauty. In other words, a person's affections may transmigrate from one object of desire to another. And yet this is futile because 'all men are pursuing a shadow, the Unattainable'.

The story is set on the 'Isle of Slingers' (Portland Island in South Dorsetshire: a long peninsula stretching several miles out into the sea), and its hero is the twenty-year-old Jocelyn Pierston (sometimes spelt Pearston, by Hardy), who is a sculptor. Pierston's 'well-beloved' was

> perhaps of no tangible substance [but rather] a spirit, a dream, a frenzy, a conception, an aroma, an epitomised sex, a light of the eye, a parting of the lips. He [Pierston] knew that he loved the Protean [i.e. variable, taking many forms] creature wherever he found her, whether with blue eyes, black eyes, or brown.[1]

Given Hardy's own particular circumstances, it is easy to imagine that through the novel, he was living his life vicariously through the character of Pierston. For example, during his courtship of Emma, Hardy's 'Well-beloved' would undoubtedly have found its embodiment in her. However, when severe and intractable problems arose in their relationship, such as have already been alluded to, Hardy's 'well-beloved' may have migrated, perhaps to one or more of the aforementioned society beauties whom he was constantly encountering when in London – for instance, Florence Henniker, and the beautiful Lady Agnes Grove.[2]

Meanwhile, in January 1897, Hardy wrote to Florence Henniker expressing his admiration for the poet Percy Bysshe Shelley (1792-1822). Of all the men whom he (Hardy) would like to meet 'in the Elysian fields', he would choose Shelley, not only for his 'unearthly, weird, wild appearance & genius', but for his 'genuineness, earnestness, & enthusiasms on behalf of the oppressed'. Surely, Hardy was a kindred spirit of that great poet.[3]

In that year, the Hardys departed from their usual routine of renting accommodation in London and instead, opted to stay at Basingstoke, 50 or so miles away, and commute to the capital every few days. In June, the month of the celebrations of Queen Victoria's Diamond Jubilee, they travelled to Switzerland to escape the crowds. On their return they visited Wells and its Cathedral; the ancient ruins of Stonehenge, and Salisbury, where they attended a service in the Cathedral.

Hardy's prodigious efforts on the literary front did not prevent him from taking a keen interest in local architectural affairs. In September he advised Hugh Thackeray Turner concerning necessary repairs and maintenance to the tower of East Lulworth church, and in October on the re-thatching and re-flooring of the White Horse Inn at Maiden Newton.[4] Hardy travelled to the sites on his bicycle, and having therefore incurred no expenses, he informed Turner that no repayment for his services was necessary. The writer Rudyard Kipling, joined Hardy for some of his cycling excursions: the latter having purchased a new Rover Cob bicycle.[5]

The following year, 1898, saw Hardy, now aged fifty-eight, travelling ever further afield on his bicycle, visiting such places as Bristol, Gloucester and Cheltenham; sometimes in company with Emma, and at other times with his brother, Henry. Often he would take his bicycle part of the way on the train. The advantage of possessing a bicycle, for literary people he said, was that they could travel a long distance 'without coming in contact with another mind – not even a horse's', and in this way there was no danger of dissipating one's mental energy.[6]

That February, Hardy, the incurable romantic, wrote to Elspeth Thomson (sister of the artist Winifred Hope Thomson), thanking her for her 'charming valentine' which made him feel young again. He said

> I can just remember the time when written valentines were customary – before people became so idle as to get everything, even their love-making, done by machinery![7]

In April, Hardy wrote to Edmund Gosse to tell him of a

> belief still held in remote parts hereabout, that the cattle kneel at a particular moment in the early hours of every Christmas morning [i.e. as if in prayer].[8]

In London in May, Hardy went to view the body of Mr Gladstone (the former prime minister) which lay in state in Westminster Hall, close to the Houses of Parliament 'where his voice had echoed for fifty years'.[9]

In that year of 1898, Hardy commenced a friendship with Hermann Lea, who was the only person with whom he was prepared to co-operate when it came to the creation of a guide book of 'Wessex' based on his novels. In this, Lea had the advantage of being a professional photographer.

In December 1898, Hardy's *Wessex Poems* was published by Harper & Brothers. In the main, the fifty or so poems contained in the volume were composed in the 1860s, but some were written more recently.[10] They were generally well received; some were about the Napoleonic era, others were drawn from Wessex life. However, the most interesting were those which gave insight into Hardy's state of mind during this period. In fact, given the tenor and content of these poems, it is difficult to escape the conclusion that in composing them, Hardy had in mind, once again, his disastrous marriage to Emma.

For example, in *Neutral Tones* he refers to having learnt, since his youth, 'keen lessons that love deceives'. In *Hap* he specifically mentions 'suffering' and 'love's loss', and finds himself wondering if some divine power is the cause of it.

If but some vengeful god would call to me
From up the sky, and laugh: "Thou suffering thing,
Know that thy sorrow is my ecstasy,
That thy love's loss is my hate's profiting!"

In *To Outer Nature* he reveals that the real-life Emma, and what he originally imagined her to be, were two completely different entities.

Show thee as I thought thee
When I early sought thee…

And then declares, sorrowfully,

Thy first sweetness,
Radiance, meetness,
None shall re-awaken.

In *Revulsion*, however, not only does all hope appear to have been extinguished, but it has been replaced by a sense of overwhelming bitterness and disillusionment.

Let me then never feel the fateful thrilling
That devastates the love-worn wooer's frame,
The hot ado of fevered hopes, the chilling
That agonizes disappointed aim!

So I may live no junctive law fulfilling,
And my heart's table bear no woman's name.

In fact, the very title of the poem surely sums up Hardy's sentiments at this time.

In London, as usual with Emma, in the spring of 1899, Hardy continued to fraternise with the literary set and met with the poet A. E. Housman, for the first time. That October he was present in Southampton on the occasion of the departure of troops for the South African war, and saw similar preparations being made by the battery stationed at Dorchester – events which inspired him to write several poems.

In June Hardy wrote from London to his sister Kate, asking her to remember to instruct the local carpenter to erect a cupboard outside the door of the bedroom that was formerly his study at Max Gate, and furthermore he enclosed a diagram showing exactly where this cupboard should be located.[11]

He was now writing frequently to Florence Henniker. In July he complained to her that one of the problems with life in the country was the unavailability of good music. In October, referring to the South African war, he told her how he deplored the fact that civilized nations had learnt no other way of settling disputes than 'the old & barbarous one'.[12]

Five

A NEW CENTURY

The coming of the new century, in 1900, found Hardy as energetic as ever: cycling from Max Gate all the way to Portland Bill and back in one day – a distance of 20 miles, up hill and down dale.

That February he told Florence Henniker how he was enjoying studying the strategy and tactics of the current war, but he also expressed his horror at the fate of Boer general Piet Cronje, whose army, including its womenfolk, was currently trapped in a river bed (by British forces), and whose animals were being 'mangled'.[1] Also in February, Lady Grove visited Max Gate.

In July, Hardy apprised journalist and author William Earl Hodgson, of his view that the (British) constitution 'has worked so much better under queens than kings', and recommended that 'the Crown should [therefore] by rights descend from woman to woman'.[2] So much for any suggestion that Hardy had an inherent bias against women.

During William Lyon Phelps's visit to Max Gate on 9 September 1900, Hardy admitted to him that

> *A Laodicean* contained more of the facts of his own [i.e. Hardy's] life than anything else he had ever written. [Also] He wished to be considered and remembered only as a poet. Instead of a great novelist writing verse as an avocation, he wished to be regarded as an English poet who had written some stories in prose.[3]

In October, Hardy opined to Florence Henniker that 'the present condition of the English novel is due to the paralysing effect of English criticism on those who would have developed it'.[4] Here, of course, he was speaking from bitter personal experience. He also enquired whether she had heard from her father, the colonel, currently serving in South Africa with the British army.

In that same month of October, Emma heard that her widowed sister Helen, now resident at Lee-on-Solent in Hampshire, had fallen ill. Emma left Max Gate immediately to go and care for her. Two months later, however, Helen died at the age of sixty-three.

Hardy's *Poems of the Past and Present* was published in November 1901 by Harper & Brothers of New York. The poems cover a variety of subjects: war, other writers and poets (in particular Shelley and Keats), flowers, birds, Rome, Switzerland, and there is a humorous one entitled *The Ruined Maid*.

Just as many of the happenings described in Hardy's novels had their root in his own experiences, so the same pattern emerges in his poems, where his main preoccupation appears to be his fraught relationship with Emma. And because the couple's problems remained unresolved, the outpouring of plaintive poetry never ceases. (This continued to be the case, even after Emma's death.)

In '*How Great My Grief*', Hardy appears to complain that although he has displayed love and kindness towards his wife, he feels that this has not been reciprocated. Nevertheless, he has decided to accept his fate, despite the fact that the passage of the 'slow years' has brought no amelioration.

How great my grief, my joys how few,
Since first it was my fate to know thee!
– Have the slow years not brought to view
How great my grief, my joys how few;
Nor memory shaped old times anew
Nor loving-kindness helped to show thee
How great my grief, my joys how few,
Since first it was my fate to know thee?

Similarly, in '*I Said to Love*', he writes of that latter subject as follows.

It is not now as in old days
When men adored thee and thy ways...

And continues

I said to him,
"We now know more of thee than then;
We were but weak in judgement when,
With hearts abrim,
We clamoured thee that thou would'st please
Inflict on us thine agonies..."

Having thus implied that it had been a misjudgement on his part to marry Emma, Hardy goes on to refer to 'iron daggers of distress', but says, resignedly, 'We are too old in apathy' to fear any further threats from 'Love'. The inference is clear. Hardy once longed for love, but is now totally disillusioned with the hand that fate has dealt him.

In *To Lizbie Browne*, Hardy laments the fact that the eponymous subject of the poem had eluded him.

When, Lizbie Browne,
You had just begun
To be endeared
By stealth to one,
You disappeared
My Lizbie Browne.

And he continues:

You were a wife
Ere I could show
Love, Lizbie Browne.

In other words, soon after his meeting with Lizbie, she had gone off and married somebody else. In real life, Lizbie Browne was the beautiful, red-headed daughter of a local gamekeeper, who was known to Hardy in his youth. The inference of the poem is obvious. Hardy, in retrospect, feels that it was *she* he ought to have married. Instead, he let her slip, when he should have 'coaxed and caught' her, 'ere you [she] passed'.

If, as appears to be the case, Hardy found it impossible to maintain a normal physical and emotional relationship with his wife Emma, how did he himself manage to maintain any semblance of normality, either emotionally or physically? For example, would he not have found life to be immensely frustrating on both counts?

What was not known in Hardy's time is that during orgasm, as experienced during sexual intercourse, endorphins (substances produced by the pituitary gland which are related to the opiate morphine) are released which create both a feeling of euphoria, and also have an analgesic effect. It should be noted that endorphins are also released during strenuous or prolonged physical exercise, such as cycling. Hardy was a keen cyclist and this activity was therefore undoubtedly beneficial to his health and well-being, even if it in no way compensated him for enforced sexual abstinence.

Hardy might have found it helpful to discuss his feelings with loved ones and friends, but a), his reticent nature would probably not have permitted him to do so and b), Emma did not welcome his family into her home, and would have objected strongly to any acquaintance of Hardy visiting Max Gate for that purpose. This avenue was therefore denied to him. As for consulting his doctor about the depression, from which he undoubtedly suffered from time to time, there is no record that he ever went so far as to do this.

The fact that Hardy became more and more depressed during his marriage to Emma is reflected in his writings. Compare, for example, the happy scenes portrayed in *Under the Greenwood Tree* (written in 1871, three years prior to his marriage), with the harrowing and heart-rending scenes portrayed in *Jude the Obscure* (written in the seventeenth and eighteenth years of his marriage). But was his physical health also affected adversely? From his letters, it is evident that Hardy suffered continually with head colds and rheumatism, in London and in Dorsetshire, and also with dyspepsia; though whether or not this was stress related cannot be said with certainty.

Six

LIFE GOES ON: *THE DYNASTS* TAKES SHAPE: *TIME'S LAUGHINGSTOCKS*

William Archer visited Max Gate in February 1901, when Hardy stated to him as follows.

When I was quite a young man, an architect's pupil, I used to be sent round to sketch village churches as a preliminary to their restoration – which mostly meant destruction. I feel very remorseful now; but, after all, it wasn't my fault – I was only obeying orders.[2]

In May, to celebrate the peace agreement signifying the end of the South African war, Hardy flew a flag (presumably the Union flag) in the garden of Max Gate.[3] Later that year he remarked on how motor cars were

> rather a nuisance to humble roadsters like me, one never knowing whether the occupants are Hooligan-motorists or responsible drivers.[4]

(Hardy continued to rely on his bicycle and did not possess a car.)

On New Year's Eve 1901, Hardy pronounced upon how an individual should determine his own modus vivendi. *'Let every man make a philosophy for himself out of his own experience,'* was his advice.[1]

During the latter part of 1902, Hardy was to be found working on Volume 1 of *The Dynasts* – a story which had been taking shape in his mind over a number of years. For this he moved location yet again, into the (third) study which had been built above the newly-constructed kitchen in 1894/5.

In early 1903, Hardy remarked upon 'the decay of Parliamentary government' – a sentiment which might apply equally well today![5]

Vivisection was another topic on which Hardy gave his opinion. Although he disapproved of the practice, nevertheless, he felt it was a small matter in comparison with 'the *general* cruelty of man to the "lower" animals'.[6]

In March 1903 the Hardys stayed with Lady Grove at her house, Sedgehill Manor in Wiltshire. In that year, Hardy asked Macmillan, publisher of *The Woodlanders* (1887) and *Wessex Tales* (1888), to become his principal publisher. The request was accepted with enthusiasm. Not only that, but Hardy became a personal friend of the Macmillans and was invited to family garden parties.[7]

In January 1904 the first volume of *The Dynasts* was published by Macmillan.

In March 1904, Hardy reported on the loss of his oldest friend in Dorchester, the historian, antiquarian and watercolour artist Henry Moule (brother of Horace). His friendship with Moule, said Hardy, was a 'true friendship "which many waters cannot quench, nor the floods drown"'.[8] This quotation is derived from the *Song of Solomon*, 'Many waters cannot quench love, neither can the floods drown it'.

Hardy's mother Jemima, died on 3 April 1904, which was Easter Sunday. She was buried at Stinsford in the same grave as her husband. Although ninety years of age, her memory and intellect had remained undimmed. Said he

> It took me hours to be able to think & express what she had at the tip of her tongue. The gap left by her departure was 'wide, & not to be filled'.[9]

Hardy, together with his sisters Mary and Kate and his brother Henry, attended the funeral. However, Emma did not attend.

Hardy's letter-writing continued unabated throughout the years. In July 1904 he complained to Alfred Pope, brewer and former Mayor of Dorchester, about odours emanating from the town's sewerage system, which were so foul that he felt unable to invite friends to Max Gate[10] (though even if he had done so, it is debatable whether Emma would have allowed such visitors to venture beyond the threshold).

In October, Emma's brother Walter, assistant manager of the General Post Office in Maida Vale, London, died having retired only six months previously. (Walter's wife Charlotte, outlived him – dying in 1919.) With financial assistance from Hardy, Walter's son Gordon, had trained to become an architect. Walter's daughter Lilian, however, had drifted from place to place, including Max Gate, where she spent prolonged periods of time.

In April 1905, Hardy steeled himself to make the long journey north to Aberdeen in Scotland, to receive from that city's university the Honorary Degree of Doctor of Laws. In London in May, he attended a farewell banquet for the Lord Mayor and visited the theatre to see plays by Ben Jonson and George Bernard Shaw. In June he visited his old friend, the poet Swinburne at the latter's house in Putney.

A party of 200 members of the Institute of Journalists visited Hardy at Max Gate in September 1905 and were provided with tea, served from a marquee 150 feet long; the latter having been erected on the lawn especially for the purpose. It had been the members' own idea to visit Hardy, though he may not have shared their enthusiasm, having been the victim of no small amount of criticism from some of their number over the years.

In November, displaying his usual meticulous attention to detail, Hardy recorded the chronological order in which the trees were shedding their leaves that year: 'Chestnuts; Sycamores; Limes; Hornbeams; Elm; Birch; Beech.'[11]

February 1906 saw the publication of the second volume of *The Dynasts*. In London again that year, Hardy spent time at the British Museum library verifying certain facts for the final volume (III) of *The Dynasts*.

In June 1906 the Hardys attended a garden party given by King Edward VII at Windsor Castle. Now he had truly 'arrived' in society. In November the Dorsetshire Regiment, then based in India, asked him to provide them with a marching tune – stipulating that it must have local affinities and be suitable for rendition with fifes and drums. He duly obliged with an old tune of his grandfather's called *The Dorchester Hornpipe*.

In August 1906, Hardy and his brother Henry, embarked upon a cycling tour in order to visit the cathedrals of Lincoln, Ely, and Canterbury; as well as the Cambridge colleges. Henry was then aged fifty-five, whereas Hardy was eleven years his senior. This was no mean feat for a man of sixty-six.

Journalist and essayist Henry Woodd Nevinson, visited Max Gate in 1906, when Hardy, he said, gave him a conducted tour of Dorchester to see

> the Roman amphitheatre just south of the station where a woman was burnt alive not very long ago [It was actually in the year 1705!] on suspicion of having poisoned her husband. She had a lover, and they waited for six months till her baby was born, and then they burnt her alive in the middle of the grassy amphitheatre. On an old plan of Dorchester, Hardy also pointed out to me the hardly distinguishable spots where gallows were marked. The subjects [which included the exploits of the local hangman] have for him a horrible fascination that comes of extreme sensitiveness to other people's pain. I suppose that if we all had that intensity of imagination we should never do any harm to any human being or animal or bird, certainly not in cruelty.[12]

In February 1907, Emma went to London to join the suffragist procession. Hardy was himself in favour of women's suffrage, as he subsequently confirmed in a letter to the leader of its movement, Millicent Fawcett.[13]

In March 1907, having enlisted the support of Florence Emily Dugdale in helping him to research his books, he wrote to her to advise, that if she was 'not *quite* well', to refrain from carrying out searches (which she was doing on his behalf for *The Dynasts*) at the British Museum.[14]

Florence Dugdale (born 12 January 1879 and therefore thirty-eight years Hardy's junior) was the daughter of Edward Dugdale, headmaster of St Andrew's National School, Enfield, Middlesex and his wife, Emma. Having practised as a qualified teacher, Florence retired on health grounds in February 1908. From 1899, she had written a children's column for her local

Enfield Observer. She subsequently became a contributor to the *Standard*, the *Cornhill Magazine*, the *Daily Mail*

> and other London newspapers of the first rank; and authoress of several books for children and of short stories of considerable literary distinction.[15]

Although Florence Dugdale may have met Hardy on a previous occasion, it was allegedly in spring/summer 1905 that she first met Emma. This was at London's Lyceum Club (or to give it its full title, The International Lyceum Club for Women Artists and Writers, founded in 1904) of which Emma was a member of the Organizing Committee. On this occasion, Florence approached Emma, seeking permission to send her husband Hardy, whose writings she admired, some flowers for his birthday. In August 1905, Florence wrote to Hardy from Weymouth to enquire whether she might call on him at his home. The request was granted,[16] and in company with Florence Henniker (who was an acquaintance of hers), she duly visited Max Gate. Florence would go on to play and increasingly important part in Hardy's life.

The third and last volume of *The Dynasts* was published in February 1908. The Hardys spent that spring and summer in London, where they met Irish dramatist and critic George Bernard Shaw and his wife Charlotte, it is believed for the first time.[17]

The Dynasts: A Drama of the Napoleonic Wars, in Three Parts, Nineteen Acts, and Thirty Scenes, is the longest dramatic composition in English literature. In *The Dynasts,* and possibly again with his failed marriage in mind, Hardy would address the question of whether supernatural forces have an influence on events taking place on earth. It commences in 1805, with Napoleon's threat to invade England; covers the Battle of Trafalgar; the war in the Spanish Peninsula; Napoleon's Russian Campaign, and finally, the Battle of Waterloo where the great French commander is defeated by the Duke of Wellington. Many characters are featured: among them Lord Nelson and William Pitt. It may be argued that of even greater importance are the 'spirits', which Hardy describes as 'supernatural spectators of the terrestrial action'. They include: the 'Spirit of the Years'; of the 'Pities'; of 'Rumour'; and the spirits 'Sinister' and 'Ironic'. The 'Shade of the Earth' and the 'Angels' provide the chorus.

Hardy's 'Spirits' appear to reflect the various viewpoints of a 'normal' onlooker to what is happening on the Earth below, rather than having any religious significance. The doctrines of the Spirits, however, 'are but tentative', and not intended to offer the reader a 'systematized philosophy' by which the mystery of 'this unintelligible world' might be explained.[18] Was it possible, from a study of Napoleon, to draw some general conclusions about life on Earth, and to shed light on the great unanswered questions of the 'Why' and the 'Wherefore'?

In *The Dynasts*, where Hardy postulates the existence of an 'Immanent (all-pervading, universal) Will', the words 'This Tale of Will, And life's impulsion by Incognizance' sum up the situation succinctly. The peoples of the Earth are being continually manipulated by some great force which he calls the 'Urging Immanence',[19] of which they are completely unaware; and hence, his comment that the Napoleonic Wars were brought about 'artificially'. The corollary to this is that everything that human beings experience is predetermined. But as to what motivates this 'Will', what its values are, if any, and where it has its origins, is not explained, except to say that it 'reasonest not' and is both 'Loveless' and 'Hateless' at the same time.[20] *The Dynasts*, nevertheless, ends on a note of hope:

> ... the rages
> Of the ages
> Shall be cancelled.

And the Chorus sings out, 'deliverance' will be 'offered from the darts that were...', so that finally, 'Consciousness the Will informing' will finally 'fashion all things fair'. In other words, the 'Will' will make sure that everything comes right in the end. (Those who regard Hardy as an inveterate pessimist, may be surprised at his having come to this conclusion.)

Hardy appears to be saying that until the universal 'Will' makes itself known to us, it is not possible for us to understand why things happen. Meanwhile, human beings will continue to act, in his words, like 'puppets', like 'the mindless minions of the spell',[21] and will continue to become enmeshed in events not of their choosing, such as war.

In 1908, Hardy was as active as ever. In London, he received a visit from Lady St Helier; dined at the Royal Academy, and attended the Mansion House for a dinner commemorating the poet, John Milton. However, because Emma felt 'too weak to undertake housekeeping up there', the Hardys did not take lodgings in London that year, as was their usual practice.[22] In Dorsetshire he was invited to attend a performance of some scenes from *The Dynasts* enacted by the Dorchester Debating, Literary, and Dramatic Society. He also paid a visit to Cambridge.

In September 1908, Hardy arranged for Emma's attic bedroom to be enlarged by increasing the size of her dormer window. The porch at Max Gate was also enlarged. Meanwhile, she departed on a visit to Calais, presumably to avoid the disruption, reappearing at Max Gate on 22 October.

In November 1908, Prime Minister H. H. Asquith offered Hardy a knighthood, but the offer was declined. Why? Perhaps for the reasons Hardy himself had given, five years previously.

> I have always thought that any writer who has expressed unpalatable, or possibly subversive views on society, religion, current morals, & many other features of the existing order of things, & who wishes to be free to express more if they occur to him, must feel hampered by accepting honours from any government.[23]

In January 1909, Hardy admitted that while writing *The Dynasts*, he had experienced 'periodic frights lest I should never live to finish the book'. In consequence, 'alas', he had 'rattled along too hurriedly [with the writing of it]'.[24] (This sentiment will ring a bell with any author over the age of about sixty-five!) That year, he was appointed a governor of Dorchester Grammar School.

When his friend, the poet Algernon Swinburne died, Hardy's rheumatism prevented him from attending the funeral, which took place on 15 April 1909. That autumn he visited more cathedral cities: this time Chichester, York, Edinburgh and Durham. In late April he was to be found advising the Stinsford Church Restoration Committee. Said he

> The only legitimate principle for guidance, is to limit all renewals to *repairs for preservation*, and never to indulge in alterations.

This was 'an interesting building, and one very easy to injure beyond remedy'. He gave detailed instructions to the committee, and included a sketch to illustrate how the replacement guttering should be applied. He could not help commenting, however, on how the erection, in about 1870, of the

> imitation Early English nave roof... in place of the good old sixteenth century waggon roof with bosses, which had become decayed

had irrevocably altered 'the proportions between the tower and the nave'. Not only that, but the 'Cholmondeley monument' (to Marcia Cholmondeley, a member of the Pitt family) had been destroyed to create a corbel.[25]

In May 1909, Hardy spoke of the good that he believed would come if women were given the vote. They would help abolish 'blood-sport', 'slaughter-house inhumanities', and 'the present blackguard treatment of animals generally'. Also, men would then feel free to knock down or rationalize 'all superstitious institutions' such as 'theologies, marriage, wealth-worship, labour-worship' and 'hypocritical optimism'.[26]

To Florence Henniker, later that year, Hardy confessed to being not in the brightest of spirits, to tell the truth. Still, who can expect to be at my age, with no children to be interested in?[27]

Time's Laughingstocks, a collection of poems by Hardy, some dating back to the mid-1860s, was published by Macmillan in December 1909. Titles include: *The Fiddler*, *The Dead Quire* (in memory of those who used to sing and play in Stinsford church), and *Former Beauties* (remembering the 'young things... we loved in years agone'). But, as always with Hardy, it is the personal poems which hold the greatest fascination. In *To Carrey Clavel*, Hardy complains

You turn your back, you turn your back,
And never your face to me,
Alone you take your homeward track,
And scorn my company.

In *Bereft*, Hardy talks of 'my lone bed'. Whilst in *He Abjures Love*, he enquires:

But after love what comes?
A scene that lours,
A few sad vacant hours,
And then, the Curtain.

The Dead Man Walking begins:

They hail me as one living,
But don't they know
That I have died of late years,
Untombed although?

Surely, the sentiments expressed in these poems, are yet another terrible indictment by Hardy of his marriage to Emma.

Seven

FROM EMMA'S STANDPOINT

The portrait painted of Emma has thus far relied largely on the testimony of her husband. But what of her own thoughts and feelings? How did she view her spouse? Although Hardy destroyed Emma's manuscript entitled *What I Think of My Husband*, some of her letters have survived, together with *Some Recollections*,[1] and a portion of her *Diaries*. So she may speak for herself in her own words.

Emma described the home in Plymouth where she was brought up as

> a most intellectual one and not only so but one of exquisite home-training and refinement – alas the difference the loss of these amenities and gentilenesses has made to me.[2]

She went on to describe her dancing lessons and the pretty dresses which she wore to parties, where 'the military and navy [were] usually present'.[3] She made her disdain for Hardy quite clear, for example, when she told Edward Clodd that

> A man who has humble relations shouldn't live in the place where he was brought up.[4]

And subsequently, with his relatives in mind, she referred scathingly to 'the peasant class'.[5] Here, it will be recalled that Hardy wrote his first novel *The Poor Man and the Lady*, in the year 1867, whereas he first met Emma in 1870. Therefore, he was preoccupied with feelings of inadequacy, in regard to his social status, well before he first met her, and she merely reinforced these feelings in him. In November 1894, Emma had complained that Hardy's interest in the cause of women's suffrage was 'nil': 'He understands only the women he *invents* – the others not at all.'[6]

In a letter to Mary Hardy (currently headmistress of Dorchester's National School for Girls), dated February 1896, Emma launched a diatribe of invective.

> I dare you, or any one to spread evil reports of me – such as that I have been unkind to your brother, (which you actually said to my face,) or that I have 'errors' in my mind (which you have also said to me), and I hear that you repeat to others.
>
> Your brother has been outrageously unkind to me – which is *entirely your* fault: ever since I have been his wife you have done all you can

to make division between us; also, you have set your family against me, though neither you nor they can truly say that I have ever been anything but just, considerate, & kind towards you all, notwithstanding frequent low insults.

As you are in the habit of saying of people whom you dislike that they are 'mad' you should, & may well, fear, least [1est] the same be said of you... it is a wicked, spiteful & most malicious habit of yours.

You have ever been my causeless enemy – causeless, except that I stand in the way of your evil ambition to be on the same level with your brother by trampling upon me... doubtless you are elated that you have spoiled my life as you love power of any kind, but you have spoiled your brother's & your own punishment must inevitably follow – for God's promises are true for ever.

You are a witch-like creature & quite equal to any amount of evil-wishing & speaking – I can imagine you, & your mother & sister on your native heath raising a storm on a Walpurgis night [the eve of 1 May when witches are said to convene and hold revels with the devil].[7]

Mary Hardy.
Photo: The National Trust

This letter may have had a basis of truth, insofar as Mary may, in her exasperation at the situation which pertained at Max Gate, have been critical of Emma and expressed this criticism to her face. However, Emma's extreme language, and the fact that her letter relates not only to Mary but to her sister Kate and her mother Jemima – all thoroughly respectable people – is evidently more a reflection of the former's mental state than of the actual situation on the ground. More will be said about this shortly.

Emma subsequently elaborated further, on the subject of witches:

Well you know they always live on *Heaths*, or Moors or desolate plains or Mountains – but have no mediaval [sic] ways or any broom-sticks etc, but are *modern* evil-*wishers* as the name means... [and] they can throw the odium of their evil doings & wishings on the innocent. There are, as a matter of fact, many malicious defamers *here* in, ah even, in 'Casterbridge' [Hardy's name for Dorchester].[8]

Another of Emma's fears – a more rational one this time – was that the French would invade England and enforce the Catholic faith. As might be guessed, Emma was fervently anti-Catholic. For this reason, at Max Gate she always kept a suitcase filled with provisions to hand, so that should the necessity arise, she could immediately take flight.[9]

By February 1897, Emma's comments about Hardy had become increasingly acidulated. Said she

> One thing I abhor in Authors. It is their blank materialism… I get irritated at their pride of intellect.[10]

In August 1899, in another thinly veiled criticism of her husband, she said

> I can scarcely think that love proper, and enduring, is in the nature of men. There is ever a desire to give but little in return for our devotion, & affection.

And she warned

> Interference from others is greatly to be feared - members of either family too often are the cause of estrangement.[11]

In November 1902 Emma, in another reference to Hardy, declared

> I fear I am prejudiced against authors – living ones! – they too often wear out other's lives with their dyspeptic moanings if unsuccessful – and if they become eminent they throw their aider over their parapets to enemies below, & revenge themselves for any objections to this treatment by stabbings with their pen![12]

This comment by Emma leaves no doubt that she was aware Hardy was making, what she considered to be, disparaging allusions to her in his writings. Meanwhile, her criticisms of him continued unabated. In April 1910, for example, she stated

> I have my private opinions of men in general & of him in particular – grand brains – much 'power' – but too often, lacking in judgment of ordinary matters – opposed to *un*selfishness – as regards them*selves*! – utterly useless & dangerous as magistrates! [a position which Hardy held] & such offices – & to be put up with until a new order of the universe *arrives*, (IT WILL).[13]

As far as Christianity was concerned, it must have been a source of great regret to Emma, who had been brought up in a church-going family, and whose mother 'read the Bible with exceeding diligence', that her husband did not share her beliefs. Nevertheless, her faith was undimmed, for in

January 1911 she opined that

> an Unseen Power of great benevolence directs my ways; I have some philosophy and mysticism, and an ardent belief in Christianity and the life beyond this present one... Outward circumstances are of less importance if Christ is our highest ideal.[14]

Emma donated money to various Christian charitable institutions, including the Salvation Army and the Evangelical Alliance. Also, it was her habit to have pamphlets printed, which she left in local shops or at the homes of people she visited. The purpose of these 'beautiful little booklets', as she described them (in her own, somewhat ungrammatical language), was to

> help to make the clear atmosphere of pure Protestantism in the land to revive us again – in the *truth* – as I believe it to be.[15]

Eight

WHAT OTHERS THOUGHT OF EMMA: A PROVISIONAL DIAGNOSIS OF HER CONDITION

It would be easy to dismiss Hardy's diagnosis of Emma's condition, that of 'madness', simply as sour grapes on his part. She refused to have a sexual relationship with him; he would therefore revenge himself by denigrating her character. But Hardy was not the only person to realize that there was something fundamentally awry with his wife's make up. For example, Hardy's fellow author, (Francis) Mabel Robinson, writing of Emma in the spring of 1891, said that her 'thoughts hopped off like a bird on a bough'.[1]

Christine, daughter of George Wood Homer and Eliza (née Sturdy) of Athelhampton Hall and a friend of the Hardys, described how one day, when she was a girl, Emma arrived at her house and asked if she might see her pet rabbits, guinea pigs and birds. Instead of looking at any of the animals, Emma 'spent the whole time watching the flies on the window panes' and expressing 'enthusiastic delight at the sweet way in which they washed their little faces and stroked their pretty wings'. When Christine was aged sixteen, Emma invited her to accompany her by train on a visit to Parkstone, to see a friend who had 'an aviary of foreign birds' in her garden. They arrived at the friend's house and viewed the birds together. Whereupon Emma, ignoring Christine altogether, withdrew to the drawing room, where she and her friend read poetry to one another. When it was time to catch the train home, Emma travelled first class and left Christine to travel third class.

If a visitor arrived at Max Gate, said Christine, and Emma suspected that the person had 'no interest in or friendship for her, but had come only to see Mr Hardy and worship at his shrine', she would not inform her husband of the presence of that visitor, who would go away 'without seeing his hero'.

Emma 'would have liked to have received the admiration of the world for talents she believed she possessed', but, according to Christine, the poems she wrote were 'indifferent', and as for her talents, they were 'not discernable to anybody else'. Christine states that nevertheless, Emma

> had the fixed idea that she was the superior of her husband in birth, education, talents, and manners. She could not, and never did, recognize his greatness.

In other words, Christine believed Emma to be deluded, in respect of her opinion of herself.

Christine described Emma as 'a peculiar woman.

> She was an increasing embarrassment to her husband. She sought an attention from the world which she never received. It may well be that she was deserving a pity and compassionate understanding rather than blame. At first she had only been childish, but she got steadily worse with advancing age and became very queer and talked curiously. In her younger days she had been pleasant, but never brainy.

Finally, it had been 'a burdensome grief' to Hardy that Emma 'had not cared for any of his family'.[2]

It was not only friends, acquaintances and employees who remarked on Emma's bizarre behaviour, but also her own relatives. For example, 'Leonie' (Leonora Randolph) Gifford, Emma's second cousin, visited Emma in 1910 on an occasion when a person of some importance was expected for tea. The visitor failed to arrive, but despite this, Leonie was offered no tea herself.[3]

Lorna Stephanie Heenan was the daughter of Dr Frederick B. Fisher, who (until he retired in 1910) was Hardy's medical adviser. Lorna stated that Emma's

> mental condition progressively deteriorated, with a consequential increased strain on her husband. [Also] Her 'heretical' outbursts in the local papers caused her husband great embarrassment.[4]

As for Dr Fisher himself, he was of the opinion that Emma was 'the cause of much of the great man's pessimism and depression'.[5]

Evelyn L. Evans was the daughter of Mr Alfred H. Evans: by day a pharmacist, but by night a producer of Hardy's plays for the Dorchester Debating, Literary and Dramatic Society. From an early age, Evelyn, who had been taught to 'reverence' Hardy, described the 'mauve, satin ribbons' that used to wave from Emma Hardy's bonnet as she bicycled around the town. 'She was considered very odd by the townspeople [of Dorchester],' said Evelyn, who would 'touch their foreheads significantly as she went by, free-wheeling... with her feet off the pedals'. According to Evelyn, during Emma's latter years

> her delusions of grandeur grew more marked. Never forgetting [that] she was an archdeacon's niece [a reference to Emma's uncle, the Reverend Edwin Hamilton Gifford, Archdeacon of London, who had conducted Emma's marriage ceremony], who had married beneath her she was heard to say in front of guests, 'Try to remember, Thomas

Hardy, that you married a lady.' She persuaded embarrassed editors to publish her worthless poems, and intimated that she was the guiding spirit of all Hardy's work.[6]

Emma Hardy in her late sixties, with cat 'Snowdove'.
Photo: The National Trust

Edward Clodd described the 'absurd' way in which Emma dressed as reminiscent 'of some nymph in a picture by Botticelli'. (Clodd's assertion is amply borne out by contemporary photographs taken of Emma.)[7]

Publisher Sir Newman Flower declared that Emma became 'eccentric', and

> would leave an open copy of the Bible [permanently] on the dressing-tables of the guests' bedrooms'. [The page might be] thick with dust before the next visitors arrived, but the message was there to be read.[8]

In Flower's opinion, she exhibited 'a mild form of religious mania'.

The writer A. C. Benson, and Edmund Gosse visited Max Gate together on 5 September 1912. Benson, who had not met Emma before, described her as

> A small, pretty, rather mincing elderly lady with hair curiously puffed & padded [and] rather fantastically dressed. It was hard to talk to Mrs H. who rambled along in a very inconsequential way, with a bird-like sort of wit, looking sideways & treating my remarks as amiable interruptions.

As Emma showed him, 'in a curious peering way', the drawing room at Max Gate, she talked

> in a hurried voice, as if she was thinking aloud and not regarding me at all.

In the garden, Emma became obsessed with pinching the pods of the plant *noli-me-tangere* (yellow balsam) in order to make them eject their seeds.

> Mrs Hardy got entirely absorbed in this & went on doing it with little jumps and elfin shrieks of pleasure.

Max Gate.

The visit to Max Gate, said Benson, left him with

> a melancholy impression. It gave me a sense of something intolerable the thought of his [Hardy's] having to live day & night with the absurd, inconsequent, huffy, rambling old lady. They don't get on together at all. The marriage was thought a misalliance for her, when he was poor & undistinguished, and she continues to resent it.

As for Hardy, said Benson

> He is not agreeable to her either, but his patience must be incredibly tried. She is so queer, & yet has to be treated as rational, while she is full, I imagine, of suspicions & jealousies & affronts which must be half insane.[9]

Hardy himself had a degree of insight into his wife's condition. For example, on 17 December 1912, he wrote to Florence Henniker and described 'certain painful delusions' which Emma 'suffered from at times'.[10]

In April 1913, following Hardy's visit to him at his home in Aldeburgh, Suffolk, Edward Clodd recorded in his diary that he (Hardy) had

> talked about his wife. She had illusions that she was being followed by some man, that people were conspiring against her: all showing the mad strain in the family blood.[11]

In other words, Hardy was aware that not only Emma, but some other members of her 'Gifford' family, had mental health problems. The full extent of these problems will be revealed shortly.

Clodd also stated that he had been told by Hardy of

> the illusion [Emma] nursed that she had written his novels because he got her to copy his MSS [manuscripts].[12]

In both of these instances, Hardy was describing not 'illusions' (misapprehensions of the true state of affairs), but 'delusions' (false beliefs) held by his wife Emma.

In July 1913, Clodd visited Max Gate, where he was introduced to Hardy's brother Henry, whom he described as 'a well-set, sensible man', and his two sisters Mary and Kate, whom he described as 'ladylike, refined' and 'well-informed'. However, Clodd remonstrated with Hardy for allowing his 'half-mad wife' to deny his family – 'these well-bred folk as well as his mother [Jemima]' – access to Max Gate.[13]

In March 1914 (sixteen months after the death of Emma on 27 November 1912), Hardy wrote again to Florence Henniker, to say of Emma how

> during her latter years... her mind was a little unhinged at times, & she showed unreasonable dislikes.[14]

In November 1914, Hardy sent Emma's cousin, Kate Gifford, a copy of his newly published collection of poems, *Satires of Circumstance: Lyrics and Reveries*

> not because I think you will care for a large number of them, but because it contains some that relate to Emma.

And he went on to tell Kate how

> in later years an unfortunate mental aberration for which she was not responsible altered her much, & made her cold in her correspondence with friends & relatives, but this was contrary to her real nature, & I myself quite disregard it in thinking of her.[15]

In other words, Hardy was in denial about the full extent of Emma's mental disorder.

On 25 November 1914, Emma's cousin Kate Gifford, wrote to Hardy thus.

> Emma and I met at my Brother's at Blackheath not long before her death & I was so glad to see her again. It must have been very sad for you that her mind became so unbalanced latterly.[16]

The inescapable conclusion is, therefore, that Emma had significant mental health problems, which even members of her own family acknowledged, and which became progressively worse as the years wore on. Given the fact that, as far as is known, she received no psychiatric help for her condition during her lifetime, is it possible to come to a conclusion about her mental state? Modern-day psychiatrists divide such so-called 'personality disorders' into various categories:

1. Paranoid Commencing by early adulthood, sufferers exhibit

> a pervasive distrust and suspiciousness of others such that their motives are interpreted as malevolent.[17]

2. Histrionic Commencing by early adulthood, sufferers exhibit 'a pervasive pattern of excessive emotionality and attention seeking'. Such a person is

> uncomfortable in situations in which he or she is not the centre of attention.[18]

3. Narcissistic (Narcissism – otherwise known as 'egomania') – Commencing by early adulthood, sufferers exhibit

> a pervasive pattern of grandiosity, need for admiration, and lack of empathy. [They have] a grandiose sense of self-importance, [and are] preoccupied with fantasies of unlimited success, power, brilliance, beauty, or ideal love.

They believe themselves to be 'special and unique' and that they 'can only be understood by, or should associate with, other special or high-status people'. He or she requires

> excessive admiration; lacks empathy; is unwilling to recognize or identify with the feelings and needs of others; is often envious of others or believes that others are envious of him or her.

Such a person may display 'arrogant, haughty behaviour or attitudes'.[19]

4. Schizoid Commencing by early adulthood, sufferers exhibit 'a pervasive pattern of detachment from social relationships and a restricted range of expression of emotions in interpersonal settings'. He or she

neither desires nor enjoys close relationships, including being part of a family; almost always chooses solitary activities; has little, if any, interest in having sexual experiences with another person; takes pleasure in few if any, activities; lacks close friends or confidants other than first-degree relatives.[20]

5. Schizotypal Commencing by early adulthood, sufferers exhibit

a pervasive pattern of social and interpersonal deficits marked by acute discomfort with, and reduced capacity for, close relationships.

He or she may exhibit

ideas of reference [a mistaken belief that external events, such as newspaper articles, voices heard on the radio, people talking, etc., relate specifically to themselves]; odd beliefs or magical thinking that influence behaviour... (e.g. superstitiousness, belief in clairvoyance, telepathy, or 'sixth sense'); odd thinking and speech; suspiciousness or paranoid ideation; inappropriate or constricted affect [mood]; behavior or appearance that is odd, eccentric, or peculiar.[21]

The epithets 'childlike' and 'trusting' were often applied to Emma by those close to her and this may reflect the fact that she was emotionally immature. Such people will 'spend a large proportion of their lives creating situations in which they become the centre of attention' (as in Histrionic Personality Disorder – see above) in order, it is believed, to counter their own 'low levels of self-esteem and self-confidence'. However, 'the relief is temporary' because 'the underlying problem remains unaddressed'.[22]

Clearly, Emma's symptoms are not confined to just one of the above sub-groups, which is by no means unusual. After all, human beings are infinite in their variety and such categorisation was originally created perhaps more for the benefit of the doctor/psychiatrist than for the patient.

But what of Emma's delusions – a delusion being a false, personal belief which cannot be altered by reasoned argument? According to modern-day psychiatrists, an individual may experience one or more of the following types of delusion.

i. Grandiose

The central theme of the delusion is the conviction of having some great (but unrecognized) talent or insight or having made some important discovery. Grandiose delusions may have a religious content.

ii. Persecutory The person believes that

> he or she is being conspired against, cheated, spied on, followed, poisoned or drugged, maliciously maligned, harassed, or obstructed in the pursuit of long-term goals.

iii. Erotomanic A person believes that another person is in love with him or her. However, although 'erotomania' is defined as 'excessive or abnormal erotic desire: a preoccupation with sexual passion'[23]

> the delusion often concerns idealized romantic love and spiritual union rather than sexual attraction. The person about whom this conviction is held is usually of higher status.[24]

Emma evidently experienced both grandiose and persecutory delusions. As to whether she experienced erotomanic delusions, more will be said about this shortly.

Finally, because there is evidence that many, if not all, of the above types of personality disorder and delusion have a familial basis, it is pertinent to enquire as to whether any of Emma's relatives also exhibited signs of these conditions.

Nine

HARDY, EDWARD CLODD AND FLORENCE DUGDALE

Hardy had first met Edward Clodd in Aldeburgh in June 1891, since when he had made another half-a-dozen, or so, visits to his home, Stafford House. In early August 1909, Clodd invited Hardy and Florence Dugdale (but not Emma) to visit him at Aldeburgh, which they duly did, for a week or so beginning the 13th, and again, at the end of that month, and also in Spring 1910.

In April 1910, Hardy found a flat to rent at Blomfield Court, Maida Vale[1] at which he, Emma, and the servants arrived in May. In early June, Emma invited Florence to Blomfield Court, to a Hardy 'At Home'. This was followed by an invitation to her from Emma to visit Max Gate.

On 18 July 1910, Hardy wrote from Blomfield Court to Emma, who by now had returned to Dorsetshire, to say

> Miss Dugdale is coming this afternoon, if she can or tomorrow, to see that I am all right, & to put things straight preparatory to my leaving & to write some letters.[2]

Hardy and Florence visited Clodd once again, from 2-6 September. Three days later on the 9th, Florence arrived at Max Gate (until 29th), where she assisted Emma by typing up some of the latter's stories and poems, prior to them being offered to publishers. Florence visited Max Gate several more times that year, including at Christmas. In the meantime, she and Emma enjoyed an amicable correspondence.

In autumn 1909, Hardy took Florence to visit Chichester in Sussex and its Cathedral, and in March 1910 to Ventnor on the Isle of Wight. Did he regard Florence simply as a companion, as he gallivanted about the countryside with her, and as often as not without a chaperone? If so, why did he resort to subterfuge, as for example when, in June 1910, he introduced her to Irish dramatist and theatre manager Lady Gregory, as his 'young cousin'.[3]

By autumn 1910, Florence had virtually joined the Hardy household at Max Gate. However, despite this fact, Hardy continued to take her on excursions, but without Emma. For example, the pair visited Clodd again in October 1911, Weymouth in early October 1911, and Clodd again in May 1912. Was Emma cognizant of what one may assume was the real nature of these excursions? Undoubtedly not, otherwise she would certainly have forbidden Florence to join the Max Gate household.

As regards the innocence, or otherwise, of the relationship, one might be inclined to give Hardy the benefit of the doubt, were it not for the fact that, typically, he expressed his feelings for Florence in poems – three in particular. In *After the Visit*, he describes her 'large luminous living eyes'. *On the Departure Platform* begins with the words, 'We kissed at the barrier'. In the third verse, by which time Florence has made her way along the platform to her railway carriage, he writes

> That flexible form, that nebulous white;
> And she who was more than my life to me
> Had vanished quite.

In *To Meet or Otherwise*, he writes of the 'girl of my dreams', and 'maiden dear'. Surely the author of these poems was a man who had fallen in love?

Ten

FURTHER INSIGHTS: AWARDS: THE DEATH OF EMMA

Said Arthur Compton Rickett of Hardy

> I never heard him say an unkind thing about anyone. When the faults of A or B were being discussed by others, and the faults were too obvious to be denied, he was silent. Once when C's character was under discussion and Hardy was appealed to, he merely said: 'He was very kind to me.' There you have it. Anyone who had shown him kindness was immune from personal criticism.[1]

In March 1910, Hardy visited the grave of his friend, the poet Swinburne, on the Isle of Wight and composed a poem entitled *A Singer Asleep,* in his memory. On 6 May, when he and Emma were in London as usual - staying in a rented flat – there came the announcement that King Edward VII had died.

In April 1910, Hardy took Florence Dugdale to Southwold in Suffolk, where he introduced her to Florence Henniker, who had a house there. The two women subsequently became friends.

Now aged sixty-nine, Hardy was as active as ever. Advising Lady Grove about her writing, he confessed modestly

> 'that I am no authority. I have written heaps of ungrammatical sentences I dare say', and he had learnt his grammar by 'general reasoning, rather than by rules'.[2]

To Sidney Trist, editor of the publication *Animals' Guardian*, he explained how difficult it was to extend 'the principle of equal justice to all the animal kingdom', when nature herself was 'absolutely indifferent to justice'.[3]

Having been recommended for the award by Prime Minister Herbert H. Asquith, Hardy, on 19 July 1910, was duly invested with the Order of Merit by the new king, George V.[4] Said Florence

> Though he accepted the award with characteristic quietude, it was evident that this sign of official approval of his work brought him pleasure.[5]

Why, having declined a knighthood, did Hardy choose to accept the Order of Merit? Perhaps a), because it was a higher honour and b), because his focus was now on poetry, he therefore felt that he was no longer at risk from offending the 'establishment'.

When Emma returned to Max Gate, leaving him in London, Hardy wrote to her saying how depressing it was to come home late in the evening to a 'dark, silent flat' which was 'full of the ghosts of all those who have visited us there'.[6]

To journalist and newspaper editor Moberly Bell, on the subject of suffrage, Hardy opined that a woman had as much right to vote as a man, but wondered 'if she may not do mischief with her vote'. What the nature of this mischief might be, he did not specify.[7]

In August, Hardy complained to the superintendent of the Dorchester police about some boys whom the servants had caught stealing apples from his garden at Max Gate. He wished the superintendent to enquire into the matter, and 'at least caution the boys' – whose names were known to him. However, he did not wish them 'to be punished further than that… (which presumably would have meant them being birched).[8]

That November, Hardy was honoured by being given the Freedom of Dorchester – his native county town. At the ceremony, he proudly wore his Order Of Merit insignia. In December he described as 'such a loss', the death of 'Kitsey' the 'study cat', who was accustomed to sleeping 'on my writing table on any clean sheets of paper', and to be 'much with me'.[9] By this time, Florence Dugdale had become a permanent feature of the Hardy household.

The year 1911 saw Hardy energetically continuing with his programme of visits to all the English cathedrals. In April he was at Lichfield, Worcester, and Hereford. In June, together with his brother Henry, he was at Carlisle. This latter visit to the Lake District gave him the opportunity to see the grave of the poet Wordsworth, at Grasmere church and to take in Chester Cathedral on the return journey. In July, this time in company with his sister Kate, he visited Devon, where yet another cathedral was ticked off the list: that of Exeter. In November, the Dorchester Debating, Literary, and Dramatic Society staged performances of plays derived from his 'Wessex' novels.

One of the most detailed and illuminating accounts of the goings on at Max Gate was provided by Alice ('Dolly') Harvey, née Gale. 'As soon as I left school in 1911', said Dolly, who was now aged fourteen

> I watched the advertisement columns in *The Western Gazette* for a suitable job as I was very anxious to stand on my own feet. One day I saw an advertisement for female help at Max Gate, the home of Mr and Mrs Thomas Hardy in Dorchester.

However, Dolly's parents issued a caveat. They

> did not want me to work there, as locally Hardy's morals were not considered to be of the best. I was brought up in a strict home and my parents warned me to be careful in my relations with Mr Hardy and at the slightest suspicion of any doubtful behaviour on his part I was to leave the house instantly and return home.

Alice ('Dolly') Harvey, née Gale, 1914

Nonetheless, said Dolly, she 'wrote offering my services', and was duly interviewed by Hardy's wife Emma, who

> explained to me that as her health was poor and as she was getting weak she needed a personal help. My duties would include carrying her breakfast and lunch to her bedroom on the third floor, running messages for her, being available for help night and day, and brushing her hair regularly. My uniform was to be a blue dress with a white collar. I was to have every other Sunday off and a weekly half day's holiday. I was to live in at Max Gate and receive my board. I forget what the wages were.

'The terms were acceptable to me' said Dolly, 'and I gladly took the job'.

> Mrs Hardy permanently suffered from a pain in her back and constantly asked me to pat her back to give her relief. I did not know, I do not know, what her ailment was.
>
> There was always a fire burning in Mrs Hardy's bedroom on the attic floor where she habitually lived, and had her meals, only coming downstairs in the evenings for dinner. She and her husband had been 'separated' for some time, but for appearances sake still lived in the same house.
>
> For a short time her niece, Lilian Gifford, came to help, but it appeared to me that she irritated Mrs Hardy and although Miss Gifford tried hard to please, in many ways she did not come up to Mrs Hardy's standards or expectations, and one day she left in a hurry never to return during Mrs Hardy's lifetime.
>
> I was at Max Gate for about twelve months. Mrs Hardy lived entirely

separate from Mr Hardy, and I never remember him visiting her in her rooms or seeing her at all except at dinner the whole time I was there, and I never saw or heard them speak to each other. Mrs Hardy never talked to me about her husband who passed most of the day in his study. Nobody was allowed to enter this study except the housemaid to clear the fireplace and set the fire and Mr Hardy kept his eye on her the whole time. This irritated the housemaid. My impression was that Mr Hardy irritated most people and certainly all those who worked in the house. I never saw him smile. He only ever spoke to me if it was absolutely necessary and then in as few words as possible. Oh, he was a miserable old thing!

I remember being asked by him on several occasions to fetch the mail and it usually included a letter from Macmillan with MACMILLAN on the envelope. Mr Hardy never had the manners to say 'Thank you' when you fetched him anything. There was a man from Dorchester who came several times a week to look after the garden and to push Mrs Hardy in a hired bath chair for a visit to the town and to St Peter's church on Sunday. There was a cook and a housemaid in the house in addition to me, but I cannot now remember their names.

Mrs Hardy was mentally alert and I liked her very much, but I despised her husband.

And then came information which indicated that Dolly's parents' fears about their daughter's safety were well founded. Said Dolly

A maid who had worked at Max Gate before I went there told me that a pretty maid previous to her service had left because she was pregnant and claimed that it was Mr Hardy's child. This frightened me to death and I always tried to hide from him if I heard him coming. It was common knowledge in Dorchester, so I was told by my parents, as one of the reasons they did not want me to work at Max Gate, that Hardy had a mistress in London, a woman named Florence Dugdale, who had a modest reputation as a writer of childrens' tales. It was these things that worried me most rather than his supercilious manner and crooked nose both of which I disliked. I found it difficult to look at Hardy directly. If it was necessary to go to his study to see him for any reason I always focused my eyes on a plaque which he had on his desk, the words on it are indelibly inscribed on my memory as I read them over and over again 'Write, and with mine eyes I'll drink the words.'[10]

This is a quotation from Posthumus Leonatus, in Shakespeare's play *Cymbeline*:

...thither write, my queen,
And with mine eyes I'll drink the words you send,
Though ink be made of gall.

On 29 September 1911, Sir Sydney Carlyle Cockerell, director of the Fitzwilliam Museum, Cambridge, visited Max Gate. The outcome was that Hardy agreed to distribute certain of the manuscripts of his novels and poetry collections to selected libraries, both in Britain and in the USA.

On 29 December 1911, Rosamund Marriott Watson (formerly Tomson, née Ball) died at the age of fifty-one. Hardy had met her two decades earlier in the summer of 1889, when she was the wife of painter Arthur Thomson – whom she subsequently divorced in order to marry the novelist, Henry Marriott Watson. Initially, prior to realizing that Rosamund, a poet and writer, was merely making use of him in her attempt to get her work published, Hardy had become besotted by her, as his poem *An Old Likeness (Recalling R. T.)*, composed some years after her death, reveals.

Who would have thought
That, not having missed her
Talks, tears, laughter
In absence, or sought
To recall for so long
Her gamut of song;
Or ever to waft her
Signal of aught
That she, fancy-fanned,
Would well understand,
I should have kissed her
Picture when scanned
Yawning years after!

Yet, seeing her poor
Dim-outlined form
Chancewise at night-time,
Some old allure
Came on me, warm,
Fresh, pleadful, pure,
As in that bright time

At a far season
Of love and unreason,
And took me by storm
Here in this blight-time!

The sinking of the steamship RMS *Titanic* off the Grand Banks of Newfoundland in April 1912, occasioned Hardy to write a poem, *The Convergence of the Twain*, in aid of a fund for the victims. That season, instead of renting a flat in London, he and Emma elected to stay in a hotel.

At a party given by novelist, editor, and poet Ford Madox Ford, writer and journalist Douglas Goldring, described how disarmingly unpretentious and unfazed – to use a modern expression – Hardy was at being in the presence of 'high society'.

> The conversation... was no doubt very brilliant and very 'literary' but suddenly there came the usual inexplicable hush. It was broken by Hardy who, turning to an elderly lady by his side, remarked, with shattering effect, 'and how is Johnny's whooping-cough?'[11]

As seen from the viewpoint of those in whose company he now found himself, Dorsetshire was culturally little more than a primaeval swamp, and they would have greeted with incredulity, the fact that here was a person from that county, of humble origins, yet in almost every repect their superior – for example, in terms of his knowledge of music, languages, classical history, to say nothing of the fact that he was arguably, England's greatest living poet and novelist!

Harold Voss was Hardy's 'regular hired chauffeur' from 1912 to 1914 and also, after the Great (First World) War, from 1919 to 1928. Said he

> During the summer it was usual for me to drive him on Mondays and Thursdays. If a whole day trip, I called at Max Gate at 10.15 a.m. and we returned by 7.30 p.m.
>
> He preferred to be taken for drives in the remote districts away from towns and main roads. He enjoyed visiting the then unspoilt villages of the Dorset countryside. He liked an open touring car and disliked fast driving. Twenty-five miles per hour was the fastest speed he would allow me to travel. He always sat in the front with me and chatted about the places we visited, and the houses and inns we passed. During the drives he frequently spoke of incidents in his younger days, as the place or scene reminded him.

According to Voss, Hardy and his brother Henry, on their Sunbeam bicycles, had in their time, cycled all over England visiting cathedrals – in

July 1898, autumn 1909, and April 1911, for example. On the tours they had put up at village inns, and had much enjoyed drinking shandy (ginger beer and ale).

> If he had visitors he liked to take them to Bath and show them the pump room and Roman baths.

Favourite destinations for summer picnics by car were Badbury Rings, Lydlinch Common near Sturminster Newton, Stoborough, and Marnhull, where 'he had a great fondness for the Pure Drop Inn.' Ilchester in Somerset had a special attraction for him, said Voss because here was 'the site where the County Gaol once stood and criminals were hanged.'

> Very rarely would Hardy go to a café, we always had to find a village inn. Wessex accompanied him on his drives and usually Mrs Hardy.
>
> At the end of a journey Mr Hardy would give me 1/- tip, but when Mrs Hardy gave me the tip it was invariably 2/-. The old man was rather tight with his money, unlike his brother Henry who was most generous to me.[12]

On Hardy's seventy-second birthday, 2 June 1912, he was visited at Max Gate by the poets Henry Newbolt and W. B. Yeats, who had been asked by the Royal Society of Literature to present him with that society's Gold Medal in celebration of the occasion. Newbolt, in setting the scene, could scarcely disguise his discomfiture.

> The dinner lives on in my memory as beyond all others unusual and anxious. Mr and Mrs Hardy faced one another the longer way of the table: Yeats and I sat rather too well spaced at the two sides: we could hold no private communication with each other... Hardy, an exquisitely remote figure, with the air of a nervous stranger, asked me a hundred questions about my impressions of the architecture of Rome and Venice, from which cities I had just returned. Through this conversation I could hear and see Mrs Hardy giving Yeats much curious information about two very fine cats, who sat to the right and left of her plate on the table itself. In this situation Yeats looked like an Eastern Magician overpowered by a Northern Witch – and I too felt myself spellbound by the famous pair of Blue Eyes, which surpassed all that I have ever seen.
>
> At last Hardy rose from his seat and looked toward his wife: she made no movement, and he walked to the door. She was still silent and unmoved: he invited her to leave us for a few minutes, for a ceremony which in accordance with his wish was to be performed

> without witnesses. She at once remonstrated, and Yeats and I begged that she should not be asked to leave us. But Hardy insisted and she made no further appeal but gathered up her cats and her train with perfect tranquillity and left the room.

From his summary, it is clear that Newbolt had no doubt that Emma was the subject of Hardy's novel *A Pair of Blue Eyes*. He also indicated that Hardy's wife was more concerned with her cats than with the presentation of the medal to Hardy. The implication is, therefore, that Hardy asked Emma to leave the room out of fear that she would disrupt the ceremony.[13]

In July 1912, Emma gave what was to be her last garden party; and in August she made what would be her last visit to the theatre. On 22 November she felt unwell and was obliged to remain upstairs in her bedroom.

On 25 November, which was the day after Emma's seventy-second birthday, Rebekah Owen, daughter of a New York businessman and a Hardy enthusiast and her sister Catharine, arrived at Max Gate from the Lake District. Here, they were invited to tea, and Emma joined tham, despite being in great pain from her back.

The following day the doctor called and pronounced that the illness was not of a serious nature. With this news and with the assent of Emma, Hardy fulfilled a longstanding engagement that evening by attending the rehearsal of a play by local players in Dorchester. By the time he returned home at 11 p.m., Emma was asleep. The following morning, the maid informed Hardy that Emma had seemed brighter, but was now worse. Hardy went to her and found her lying unconscious. By the time the doctor arrived, she was dead.

It was Dolly Gale, Emma's personal help, who gave the most illuminating account, not only of Emma's final hours, but also of Hardy's somewhat bizarre behaviour at this time. Said she

> On the morning of what was to be the day of Mrs Hardy's death, November 27th, 1912, I entered her bedroom at about 8 a.m. She was moaning and terribly ill. Her appearance frightened me. She was so dreadfully drawn in her face. A great change had come over her since the previous evening. She did not complain but asked me to fetch Mr Hardy. I rushed downstairs to his study and asked him to come quickly as mistress was terribly ill and looked dreadful. Hardy looked at me disdainfully and after several seconds said: 'Your collar is crooked'. He remained seated and carefully and methodically arranged the things on his desk as though that was more important than directly going to his wife. However after a couple of minutes or so he followed me up to his wife's bedroom. It was apparent when he

> saw her that he was shocked by his wife's appearance as he then hurried to her bedside and said: 'Emm, Emm, do you know me, Emm' or 'Emm, Emm, don't you know me, it's Tom' – I am not now certain which of these expressions he used. Mrs Hardy was too far gone to answer him and from then until she died in less than five minutes she did not speak.
>
> I remember the coffin with Mrs Hardy lying in state at the foot of Mr Hardy's bed and it was then that a few friends came to pay their last respects.
>
> The maids were sent in charge of the cook to Genge's in Dorchester to buy new black outfits for the funeral and Hardy was very annoyed with cook as he thought the outfits should have been much less expensive.[14]

Genge & Co., of High West Street, were purveyors of 'Mantles, Costumes & Millinery'.

A few days before her death, the cause of which was given as heart failure and impacted gallstones, Emma had been involved in a violent quarrel with Hardy, she having ventured into the study into which he had retreated. Hardy believed that this quarrel had contributed to her death and forever thereafter, blamed himself.[15]

Emma was buried in Stinsford churchyard on 30 November 1912; her tomb having been designed by Hardy himself. Rebekah Owen, who attended the funeral, commented on 'the exceeding pathos' of the occasion.[16]

Soon after Emma's funeral, Hardy discovered in her room two 'book-length' manuscripts which she had written: one entitled *The Pleasures of Heaven and the Pains of Hell*, and the other, *What I Think of My Husband*. Having read them he tore out the pages, one by one, and burnt them in the fire.[17]

Dolly Gale had further revelations to make, which were not to Hardy's credit. Said she

> Another matter that Mr Hardy attended to with urgency was to send a telegraphic message to Miss Florence Dugdale, who then moved into Max Gate with inordinate haste. I thought Hardy was paying too much attention to Miss Dugdale so soon after his wife's death.
>
> I continued to work at Max Gate for about a month after Mrs Hardy's death and during most of that time I helped the housemaid. One day when we were making up the beds, as we shook out the sheets in Hardy's bedroom there in his bed were two hairpins. The maid merely snorted, but when I realised the situation I was shocked.

At first I thought that Hardy and Miss Dugdale had changed beds during the night.[18]

In early 1913, Hardy's brother Henry, moved from the Bockhampton family home to his own, purpose-built property, Talbothays Lodge. Here, he was joined by his sisters Mary and Kate from Dorchester, and by his cousin, Polly Antell.

In 1913, just after she had left school, Gertrude Adelia Bugler was cast as 'Marty South' in a dramatization by Dorchester pharmacist Alfred H. Evans, of Hardy's novel *The Woodlanders*. The performance, by the Dorchester Debating, Literary, and Dramatic Society, which had dramatized and staged Hardy's works since 1908, took place on 19-20 November at Dorchester's Corn Exchange.

Gertrude was a beauty, and needless to say, Hardy, now aged seventy-three, was immensely taken with her. Born in 1897, she was the daughter of Dorchester hotelier, restaurateur and confectioner Arthur Bugler and his wife Augusta, née Way, daughter of a dairyman. The Buglers allowed the dining room of their Central Temperance Hotel in South Street to be used for rehearsals, which were supervised by Hardy himself. More will be heard of Gertrude shortly.

Eleven

AN OUTPOURING OF POETRY

Hardy now embarked on poetry writing on a grand scale. In March 1913 he made a nostalgic visit to Cornwall, to St Juliot and to other favourite places which he had known with Emma. Calling at Plymouth on the return journey, he arranged for a memorial tablet, designed by himself, to be placed in the church where she had played the organ as a young woman. Here in the city, Hardy was particularly anxious to keep in contact with Emma's 'Gifford' cousins. Subsequently, Professor (Charles) Henry Gifford (1913-2003), Emma's third cousin, declared

> There was something he wanted to put right, and her family must see that he had cared for her more deeply than they knew.[1]

June found him in Cambridge receiving the honorary degree of Doctor of Letters (Litt.D.). In July, in London, he met Prime Minister Herbert Asquith and his wife, Margot.

In that year of 1913, Hermann Lea became a tenant (until 1920) of Hardy's former family home at Bockhampton.

On 10 February 1914, at St Andrew's church, Enfield, Hardy and the thirty-five-year-old Florence Emily Dugdale were married; the only others in attendance, apart from the vicar and an official, were Florence's father and sister, and Hardy's brother, Henry. After the ceremony the couple did not have a honeymoon, but returned home to Max Gate to begin their married life together.

Said Annie Mitchell, who three months earlier had been appointed cook

> I found Mrs Hardy [Florence] a very nice, considerate woman, but she was not strong. She started writing children's books about birds. At first she shared Hardy's study but later wrote in the drawing room.[2]

Despite the fact of having remarried, Hardy admitted that 'the romance of S. [St] Juliot abides none the less, & will if I live to be a hundred'. He derived consolation, however, from the fact that Florence had been 'a great friend of my late wife', and therefore there would be no 'rupture of continuity' in his life; something which he so abhorred. His ghost, he told the Reverend J. H. Dickinson, the current Rector of St Juliot, would haunt that place by reason of the experiences I was there blest with before my first marriage, & long before the sadness came that was a result of the slight mental aberration which occasionally afflicted my wife's latter years.[3]

Florence Emily Hardy by R. G. Eves.
Photo: Dorset County Museum

Hardy evidently regarded Florence as a kindred spirit, and hoped that 'the union of [their] two rather melancholy temperaments may result in cheerfulness'.[4]

In the spring of 1914, Hardy and Florence dined at the Royal Academy and met with friends, before leaving for Cambridge to be entertained by various 'worthy Heads & Fellows' of its university. One such person was Charles Moule (son of the late Reverend Henry Moule, vicar of Fordington), former tutor of Corpus Christi whom Hardy had known since his youth.[5]

In early summer 1914 the couple motored down to the West Country; Hardy having progressed (if that is the correct word) from bicycle to car. In fact, the car, a 'Benz', was not owned by Hardy (who never learned to drive), but by Tilley's Garage in Dorchester, which also provided the chauffeur, Harold Voss.[6] While in Plymouth, Hardy took the opportunity to answer questions about the Gifford family's burial vault; an attempt to clear up what he considered to be some loose ends from the past concerning his former wife's ancestors.

Meanwhile, Hardy co-operated with Hermann Lea to the extent of travelling around with him (as chauffeur) to the various places mentioned by him in his novels. Said Lea

> During 1914, 1915 and 1916 I had the privilege of taking Mr Hardy many thousand miles in my motor car. At first he seemed a trifle nervous, but this soon wore off, and, toward the latter part of 1916, he often assured me that motoring constituted his chief pleasure. As a general rule he sat in front with me, while Mrs Hardy sat behind, either alone, or accompanied by a friend.
>
> Many quite long journeys did we undertake, once going to Torquay and back in the day – nearly two hundred miles.

Lea also let slip this intriguing piece of information.

One day when Hardy paid me a visit he pointed out a tiny window at the back of the house that lighted the staircase. 'Smugglers,' he said, 'used to tap this window with their whips when passing at night, and when my father opened it a small keg of brandy used to be handed in.'[7]

The outcome of the Hardy-Lea collaboration was *A Handbook to the Wessex Country of Thomas Hardy* in 1905, and of *Thomas Hardy's Wessex* in 1911, both published by Macmillan.

In June 1914, Hardy was again in London, at a dinner of the Royal Institute of British Architects with which he had kept in touch throughout the years. As ever, Emma was always in Hardy's thoughts, and in a letter to Florence Henniker in July 1914, he confessed to feeling 'miserable, lest I had not treated her considerately in her latter life'.

Having returned from Stourhead in Wiltshire – where he and Florence had been guests of Sir Henry and Lady Hoare – Hardy wrote in his diary: 'August 4, 11 P.M. War declared with Germany.' Having previously managed to convince himself of 'the gradual bettering of human nature', he was astonished, disillusioned and depressed at the German invasion of Belgium, which had precipitated hostilities. Dorchester, where currently 400, or so, prisoners of war were being detained, was now 'teeming with soldiers, mostly drunk'.[8]

In November 1914, *Satires of Circumstance, Lyrics and Reveries* was published by Macmillan. Included in this volume was *Channel Firing*, a tirade against those who make war in the name of Christ.

All nations striving strong to make
Red war yet redder. Mad as hatters
They do no more for Christés sake
Than you do who are helpless in such matters.

In *God's Funeral*, Hardy indicates his absolute loss of faith, with this reference to the eponymous subject of the poem.

Mangled the Monarch of our fashioning,
Who quavered, sank; and now has ceased to be.

And yet, for Hardy, there was no joy to be found in what was for him God's demise; only sadness in regard to the matter of, 'who or what shall fill his place?' For the words 'I… long had prized' what was now 'mourned for' implies that he did, at one time, have a faith.

Other poems in the *Satires of Circumstance* collection relate to Emma. For example, in *When I Set Out For Lyonnesse* – a poem of hope, wonder and expectation – he recalls his first journey to St Juliot in 1870. In *The Torn Letter* he tells of how, despite everything, his longing for Emma never ceased.

That ache for you, born long ago,
Throbs on: I never could outgrow it.

Emma's cousin, Professor C. Henry Gifford, once said of Hardy, that all was 'delightful' in Emma

> the free generous impulse, the daring [person] that had once clambered over the rocks and galloped down steep hills, and the zest for living – came back to possess his mind.[9]

In *The Voice,* Hardy imagines that the late Emma is calling to him, to say that she has reverted to that delightful creature which he had originally perceived her to be:

Woman much missed, how you call to me, call to me,
Saying that now you are not as you were
When you had changed from the one who was all to me,
But as at first, when our day was fair.

In *Had You Wept*, he regrets her lack of emotional warmth.

Had you wept; had you but neared me with a hazed uncertain ray,
Dewy as the face of the dawn, in your large and luminous eye,
Then would have come back all the joys the tidings had slain
that day,
And a new beginning, a fresh fair heaven, have smoothed the
things awry.
But you were less feebly human, and no passionate need for
clinging
Possessed your soul to overthrow reserve when I came near;
Ay, though you suffer as much as I from storms the hours are
bringing
Upon your heart and mind, I never see you shed a tear.

And the poem ends:

And hence our deep division, and our dark undying pain.

In The Going, he describes what a shock the suddenness of her death was to him.

Why did you give no hint that night
That quickly after the morrow's dawn,
And calmly, as if indifferent quite,
You would close your term here, up and be gone.

And referring to the separate lives which they had led in their latter years at Max Gate, he asks himself why this had been so.

Why, then, latterly did we not speak,
Did we not think of those days long dead,
And ere your vanishing strive to seek
That time's renewal? We might have said,
'In this bright spring weather
We'll visit together
Those places that once we visited.'

He ends the poem:

...O you could not know
That such swift fleeing
No soul foreseeing –
Not even I – would undo me so!

The Wistful Lady, features 'A plaintive lady pale and passionless', and finally, *The Re-enactment* describes how 'in the [bed] chamber':

So came it that our fervours
Did quite fail
Of future consummation –

This may be interpreted as yet another intimation by Hardy that his marriage to Emma was never physically consummated. A host of other such poems, including *Rain on the Grave, Lament, A Dream or No, Beeny Cliff*, and *St Launce's Revisited*, all reveal the abject misery and remorse of the desolate Thomas Hardy. Today, these poems would be interpreted as a 'cry for help' on his part.

In December 1914, Hardy reported that Wessex had

developed a tendency to fight other dogs, quite to our surprise. We fancy he will get a nip from a big dog who lives near here, which will make him less bumptious![10]

Despite Hardy's devotion to Wessex, he was not entirely in denial about the dog's shortcomings! In that year, a black cooking range was installed in Max Gate's kitchen.

In 1915, Hardy decided not to have his customary 'season' in London, 'owing to the war & other circumstances'.[11]

In September he learned that a relative of his, a Lieutenant Frank George, had been killed at Gallipoli, bringing the tragedy of the conflict home to him in even sharper relief. The following month, in a letter to Charles Edwin Gifford, his late wife Emma's cousin, Hardy appealed for help in trying to piece together Emma's full, genealogical family tree.

Hardy's elder sister Mary, died on 24 November 1915 at their brother Henry's house at Talbothays. A schoolteacher by profession, her hobbies had been portrait painting and playing the organ at local churches, where she was much in demand. Hardy described her as 'almost my only companion in childhood'.[12] She was buried in Stinsford churchyard.

In June 1916, Hardy fulfilled his duty as Grand Juror at the Assizes, and attended rehearsals of scenes from *The Dynasts* by the Dorchester Debating, Literary, and Dramatic Society. Hardy was a stickler for perfection, and civil servant Edwin J. Stevens, a leading member of the company, described how, at a rehearsal, he

took charge of the violin and played the dance for us without a note of music in front of him.[13]

In that same month, Hardy made a nostalgic visit to Sturminster Newton, where he had written *The Return of the Native*. That September, he and Florence were to be found at St Juliot, revisiting the sites of his youthful romance with his late wife, Emma. Florence appears to have taken this in good part; at any rate disguising any feelings of jealousy or annoyance which she may have had. By autumn, according to Hardy, the number of German prisoners of war at Dorchester had risen to 5000. He went to see them and also visited wounded English servicemen in the local hospital.

In February 1917 the commandant of the local prisoner-of-war camp sent some prisoners to Max Gate to root up trees in order that the kitchen garden could be enlarged. Said Hardy

Nothing has made me feel more sad about the war than the sight of these amiable young Germans in such a position through the machinations of some vile war-gang or other.[14]

In March he could not contain his indignation at the 'Good-God' theory, which

> after some thousands of years of trial, [had] produced the present infamous and disgraceful state of Europe... that most Christian Continent!

As for the 'fifty meanings [which] attach to the word "God",' he said, the only reasonable one was the '*Cause of Things*, whatever that cause may be'. His own theory of God as both 'Goodless-and-Badless' (as portrayed by him in *The Dynasts*), might, he said, 'perhaps be given a trial with advantage'.[15]

In May 1917, Hardy confessed that (presumably owing to poor eyesight), he was 'compelled to write by machinery nowadays' – i.e. to use a typewriter.[34] In October, Hardy and Florence visited Plymouth, doubtless with the object of exploring the late Emma's former haunts.

Hardy and Florence at Max Gate. Photo: Dorset County Museum

Twelve

ONWARDS, TOWARDS EIGHTY YEARS OF AGE

In January 1918, Hardy declared that the glory of poetry lay in its largeness, admitting among its creators men of infinite variety.[1]

In February Florence wrote to Sydney Cockerell in respect of a biography of her husband which she was currently working on.

T. H. declares that he would never write an autobiography [and] the mere idea – or suggestion – annoys him. It would be a thousand pities if the MS were burned now. The safest plan is to say as little as possible about it until the thing is completed – as far as we are able to complete it.[2]

(The outcome was that *The Early Life of Thomas Hardy* and *The Later Years of Thomas Hardy*, both by Florence Emily Hardy, were published in 1928 and 1930 respectively by Macmillan.)

It is a measure of Hardy's fame and popularity that in the spring of 1918, such notable people as Lady Ilchester and Lady Londonderry came to visit him at Max Gate.

In that year of 1918, said Vera Mardon, during a rehearsal of his play *The Mellstock Choir*, at which she was present with her father

Hardy was most dissatisfied with the evolutions of the dancers in the dance 'The Triumph'. He took a lady as his partner and then, despite his age (seventy-seven) he nimbly demonstrated to the assembled company the correct steps and positions. Nor was the musical accompaniment, provided by one violin, to his liking. He was displeased with the tempo, and borrowing the violin he played in a lively manner all the required tunes from memory. He was what we should now call a perfectionist. Everything had to be as he wanted it to be – correct to the smallest detail.

Vera subsequently visited Max Gate where

Mr Hardy explained that he would like me to accompany him on the piano while he played old dance tunes on his fiddle. This I agreed to do, and it was the first of many such interludes. They gave him great pleasure. He never sang and only on one occasion did I hear him hum and that was the tune of 'O Jan, O Jan, O Jan'.[3] [A traditional Dorset song and dance.]

On another occasion at Max Gate, said Vera, Hardy

> led me to the piano and hummed the Wessex folk tune of 'Nancy's Fancy' to which the dances of 'O Jan!' could be performed, and then, almost apologetically, asked me if I would be so kind as to write down the tune.
>
> I still have the words and music I wrote down, and that was the way in which this old folk tune, which Hardy called a recension, was rescued from oblivion. Hardy had remembered the words and music he had heard played at his father's house, Upper Bockhampton, when he was a boy. It was an amazing feat of memory – a prodigious feat.[4]
>
> He did not speak the Dorset dialect, but could understand it and enjoyed the simple conversations in their native dialect of the Dorset peasants.[5]

In June 1918, with the Great War still in progress, Hardy gave a chilling view of what future wars would be like. This war was horrible enough, but would be 'merciful in comparison', bearing in mind that 'scientific munition-making is only in its infancy'.[6]

On 11 November 1918 at 5 a.m. an armistice with Germany was signed, and at 11 a.m. on that same day, a ceasefire came into effect, so marking the end of the Great War.

Hardy signed a petition in February 1919 in support of 'the reconstitution of Palestine as a national home for the Jewish people'. In May he was 'mainly destroying papers [presumably letters and diaries] of the last thirty or forty years' which, he said, 'raise ghosts'.[7]

On his birthday, 2 June, he took Florence and his sister Kate by car to visit one of his favourite places, Salisbury. Soon afterwards, Siegfried Sassoon arrived at Max Gate with a birthday present for him: a volume of the poems of some fifty living poets, intended as a 'tribute'.[8] Hardy confessed to Florence Henniker that he would care more about his birthdays if with every succeeding one he could see

> any sign of real improvement in the world. All development is of a material & scientific kind' [But despite this] scarcely any addition to our knowledge is applied to objects philanthropic or ameliorative.[9]

Shortly after the Great War, said Robert Harding, when he

entered and won a poetry competition held by the Dorchester Debating, Literary, and Dramatic Society, Mrs Hardy presented him with Hardy's own volume of poems – *Moments of Vision*.

Sometime later, Hardy himself, wishing me success in my literary career, gave this advice:- 'Have something to say, and if you have, you will discover a method of saying it.' By such encouragement I managed to write some thirty books for boys and was [became] editor of the *Boys Own* Paper...[10]

On 13 August 1919, Elliott Felkin, formerly an interpreter at the Dorchester prisoner of war camp, visited Stinsford Church where Hardy

showed me the monument of Lora Pitt [née Grey, wife of George Pitt, 1663-1734, of Kingston Maurward]; and exactly where he used to sit, on the inside next to the wall, being a little boy, and just under the carved skeleton; and said how, as the afternoon service went on and there were only the two candles in the pulpit, he used to get so frightened, looking up into its jaw.[11]

Meanwhile, on 10 August 1919 Florence wrote to Louise Yearsley (whose surgeon husband, Macleod, four years previously had performed an operation on her nose), to say

I have to go to Town [London] to see a Miss [Lilian] Gifford – niece of the first Mrs T. H. She has gone off her head, poor thing, & been put in an asylum, & I am going to see her as my husband is really not fit for the journey [in] this weather. He is rather attached to her as she lived here as a child for some years – & she has stayed with us from time to time since we were married. She was always a *most* difficult person to live with – but now I understand that the poor woman could not really help her trying ways & temper.[12]

[The institution referred to above is the London County Council's Claybury Asylum, to which, as previously mentioned, Lilian had been committed.]

It is to Florence's credit that she was prepared, in all the circumstances, to make this visit to 'poor Lilian', as she now described Emma's niece. Florence subsequently wrote to Sydney Cockerell to tell him about her visit. Said she, in regard to Lilian

I did not perceive any particular symptom of insanity, but the doctor and the medical superintendent assured me that she *was* insane.

And she proceeded to tell Cockerell how, when she was at Claybury, she had met Lilian's brother Gordon, who

> told me that he and his wife [Violet] had had a dreadful time with her [during] the last few years.

Gordon also informed Florence that Lilian had regarded Violet, a mere dressmaker, as someone 'not fit to associate' with her; that there had been

> continual scenes and unkindness... and that absurd obsession about the grandeur [presumably delusions of grandeur, on Lilian's part] of the Gifford family.

Finally, the medical superintendent had told Florence that 'from what he knew of the case, she [Lilian] can never have been quite sane'. Lilian was evidently very unhappy at Claybury, for she begged Florence to 'take her out'. However, this Florence was unable to do without the consent of the authorities.[13]

In September 1919 Florence complained to Cockerell that Hardy

> has just paid £10 for altering the tomb of the first Mrs T. H. and yet he will not buy himself a thread of clothing and he upsets himself about trifles of household expenditure involving only a few pence.[14]

Hardy continued to demonstrate his endless fascination with the legal system by attending (with Florence) the Dorchester Assizes. On 18 November, the birthday of his late father, Hardy visited the former's grave. In December he opened the Bockhampton Reading Room and Club, which would be that village's memorial to the fallen. In his speech on that occasion, he reminisced about the 'poor-houses', where parish paupers were accommodated before the workhouses were built.

In a letter which he sent to Emma's cousin, Charles Edwin Gifford, in early November 1919, Hardy revealed that his former sparkle had returned. Gifford had evidently sent him congratulations for his eightieth birthday – prematurely as it transpired, to which the latter had replied

> Many thanks for your congratulation. But it is rather amusing that, though I have been eighty in America for several years, & am now called eighty in England, I shall not really be eighty till the middle of next year [i.e. 2 June 1920], when people will doubtless begin to say: 'How many more times is that Hardy going to be fourscore!'[15]

Hardy and Florence spent the afternoon of Christmas Day 1919 at Talbothays, the home of Hardy's brother Henry, and his sister Kate, who in spring 1915 had relocated there from Dorchester to live with him.[16]

Hardy in the drawing room at Max Gate.
Photo: Reproduced by permission of the Provost and Fellows of Eton College

With the coming of the new year, accolades followed, thick and fast. In February 1920 Hardy was in Oxford to receive the honorary degree of Doctor of Letters. Robert Graves, who was present at the degree ceremony, declared

> The Sheldonian Theatre has seldom seen such enthusiasm as when Hardy came forward to be presented to the Vice-Chancellor, and was introduced in Latin as 'easily the greatest of living English novelists, nay, indeed, of English poets too,' and was invested in his gown of cardinal red. But perhaps he was even more pleased with the performance of his *Dynasts* by the Oxford University Dramatic Society that same day, and the reception that followed.[17]

In March he was elected Honorary Fellow of the Royal Institute of British Architects. April saw him visiting London for what would be the last time, when he and Florence attended Harold Macmillan's wedding to Lady Dorothy Cavendish at St Margaret's, Westminster. Macmillan's grandfather, Daniel (with brother Alexander), had founded the publishing firm of that name (which, as already mentioned, had published a number of Hardy's works), and his father, Frederick, was its chairman. The month of May saw Hardy at Exeter with Florence and Kate, attending a service at the Cathedral and calling on friends. In a letter to author and critic Harold Child, he admitted to being

> most averse to anything like an 'interview', and have been for many years.[18]

Hardy's fundamental reluctance to acknowledge people, other than friends or those who had made an appointment to see him, remained a feature of his make up. Said his cleaning lady Margaret Male

> He would never recognise the people who worked for him if he passed them in the street. I remember on several Sundays when I was out for a walk with my husband to Came Wood (a favourite walk of Hardy's, too). If Hardy was sitting on a stile or walking, he would always deliberately turn away as we passed, so as not to have to recognise or speak to us. He gave me the impression of a very shy man.[19]

A less charitable view might be that Hardy was 'stuck up' and antisocial! In May 1920 Florence stated that

> on Sundays we nearly always go to see his [Hardy's] brother & sister. [i.e. at Talbothays]

On 2 June 1920, the occasion of Hardy's eightieth birthday, he received a deputation from the Society of Authors, a member being John Galsworthy, whose works Hardy greatly admired. Those who sent congratulatory messages included the King, the Prime Minister, the Vice-chancellor of Cambridge University and the Lord Mayor of London.[20]

In August 1920, Robert Graves, with his wife Annie (née Nicholson) paid his first visit to Max Gate, where Hardy

> talked about the string-orchestras at Wessex churches, in one of which his father, grandfather, and he himself had taken part; and regretted their disappearance.
>
> That night at dinner he grew enthusiastic in praise of cyder [sic], which he had drunk since a boy, as the finest medicine he knew.
>
> He described his war-work, rejoicing to have been chairman of the Anti-Profiteering Committee, and to have succeeded in bringing a number of rascally Dorchester tradesmen to book. 'It made me unpopular, of course,' he admitted, 'but it was a hundred times better than sitting on a Military Tribunal and sending young men to the war who did not want to go.'[21]
>
> He began complaining of autograph-hunters and their persistence. He asked me for my advice and was grateful for the suggestion that a mythical secretary should reply offering his autograph at one or two guineas, the amount to be sent to a hospital ('Swanage Children's Hospital', put in Hardy), which would forward a receipt.
>
> Talk of autograph-hunters led round to professional critics. He regarded them as parasites no less noxious than autograph-hunters, and wished the world rid of them.[22]

When *The Return of the Native* was performed in Dorchester from 17-20 November 1920, Gertrude Bugler was cast as Eustacia Vye. In the same month, Hardy expressed a view with which many will concur: that 'English', as the name of this country's people, should be insisted upon, and not

> the vague, unhistoric, and pinchbeck title of 'British'.[23]

In December he modestly described his philosophy merely as

> a confused heap of impressions, like those of a bewildered child at a conjuring show.[24]

That Christmas, the carol singers came to Max Gate, as was the tradition. To Sydney Cockerell on 26 December, following a visit to Max Gate by the mummers – actors in a traditional masked mime or folk play, who had performed the *Play of Saint George* – Florence declared

> Miss Bugler looking prettier than ever in her mumming dress. T. H. has lost his heart to her entirely, but as she is soon getting married I don't let that cast me down *too* much.[25]

On 30 December Florence informed Louise Yearsley that

> we have had a rather lively Christmas in one way & another – so many people having desired to pay their 'respex' to T. H. I estimate that between 50 & 60 people have been in this house, as guests, since Christmas Day.

The fact that Hardy 'sat up' to see the New Year in may perhaps indicate in him a more contented, if not happier, frame of mind. What a contrast this was to the era of Emma.[26] In April 1921, however, Florence generously acknowledged how his late wife, in her lifetime, had helped Hardy with his work.

> Emma did indeed frequently copy for him any pages that had many alterations. She liked doing it.[27]

Scottish novelist and dramatist James Matthew (J.M.) Barrie, described a visit to Max Gate on 11-12 May 1921, in company with his secretary Cynthia, Lady Asquith, who stated as follows.

> Like so many others who have excelled in one branch of literature, he, who had excelled in two, had set his heart on writing a successful play, an ambition never realized, for all his dramatisations of his own books proved disappointments. He spoke with wistful respect for that mysterious 'sixth sense' of Barrie's – the sense of the stage which he said he was sure he did not himself possess.
>
> Barrie talked much of Hardy. 'That man couldn't look out of a window without seeing something that had never been seen before'.

Lady Asquith described Hardy's study as 'bare, simple, workmanlike and pleasantly shabby'.

> Soon after breakfast, Hardy took Barrie and me for a long walk. At over eighty he still had the stride and figure of a young man – we could scarcely keep up with him – and when he came to a hill he quickened his pace.[28]

The death of Charles Moule, the last of the Reverend Henry Moule's seven sons, occurred on 11 May 1921. In June, Hardy and Florence travelled to Sturminster Newton for a performance of *The Mellstock Quire* in the castle ruins. In July a company arrived in Dorchester preparing to make a film of *The Mayor of Casterbridge*. That same month in Dorchester, Hardy attended morning service at the church of St Peter, and opened a bazaar in aid of the County Hospital.

St John G. Ervine said of Hardy, whom he first met in 1921

> The deepest impression he made on me was of great serenity of mind, and I should describe him as a stoic who faced existence with courage and fortitude. He didn't ignore pain, but neither did he ignore pleasure. His novels are full of characters who contend with calamity and are not daunted by disaster.
>
> He was uncommonly courteous, though he let no one take liberties with him…, and he was the only great man I have ever met who seemed to have no fads except perhaps his objection to being touched. [This facet of Hardy's character will be discussed shortly.] His conversation was good without being brilliant, and he was always at his best with one or two people that he knew well. A large company silenced him. He didn't fade out of such a group, he withdrew from it, although he was still there.[29]

On 14 October 1921, poet John Masefield presented Hardy with *The Triumph*, a wooden model sailing ship which he had made himself. Masefield said of Hardy that he appeared to draw

> from inexhaustible ancestral memory… He had told a friend that he had material for another thirty years. He was in touch with a source that is undying.[30]

Hardy may have exchanged his mode of transport from a bicycle to a motor car, but in other respects he continued to display great energy. For example, he remained a prodigious letter-writer. Those with whom he corresponded included friends, eminent authors, poets, members of the Macmillan family, distinguished university academics, members of the Gifford family, together with inquisitive media correspondents anxious for him to explain aspects of the behaviour of his characters, and to reveal the locations in which his novels were set.

Thirteen
LATE LYRICS AND EARLIER

Late Lyrics and Earlier was published by Macmillan in May 1922. However, some of the poems in this collection – as the title implies – had been written several years prior to this date.

In the Preface, Hardy expressed his disappointment that the proposed revisions to the Church of England's *Book of Common Prayer* had not been 'in a rationalistic direction'. According to his wife, Florence, from that time onward

> he lost all expectation of seeing the Church [as] representative of modern thinking minds.[1]

(In the event, the revisions to which he referred were rejected by the House of Commons in 1927, and again in 1928.)

The fact that the poems included in this volume, unlike many of their predecessors, are less morbid, and display less nostalgia for years past, are a further indication that Hardy had now become somewhat less dissatisfied with life. Some of them, in fact, are quite jolly; for example, *Weathers*.

> This is the weather the cuckoo likes.
> And so do I...

Hardy's new lease of life is entirely attributable to the presence of Florence, though as already indicated, it is doubtful whether he ever acknowledged this fact. For him, the past, and Emma, and thoughts of what might have been, were never far from his thoughts. In *Faintheart in a Railway Train* he speaks of a lost opportunity to introduce himself to a 'radiant stranger' – female, of course – encountered on a station platform. In *The West-of-Wessex Girl* he regrets that the subject of the poem was 'never... squired [attended upon]' by him.

With Hardy's poems, there is a danger for the reader of not being able to see the proverbial wood for the trees – i.e. to fail to grasp the fact so many of them reflect his obsession with Emma, not only during her lifetime but also after her death.

The title of *If It's Ever Spring Again* indicates, that for Hardy, those early, happy times spent courting Emma will not come again. In *Two Serenades*, written, poignantly, one Christmas Eve, he complains that she – again, presumably, Emma – is indifferent to his overtures of love.

But she would not heed
What I melodied
In my soul's sore need –
She would not heed.

So that finally

Sick I withdrew
At love's grim hue...

In *The Rift*, Hardy refers to 'those true tones – of span so brief!'– in other words, to what he remembers as the true Emma, before her 'old gamut [musical note 'G'] changed its chime'. After this

So sank I from my high sublime!
We faced but chancewise after that,
And never I knew or guessed my crime...

Hardy could not understand why Emma had changed, and wondered if it was he who was to blame for that transformation. The truth is likely to be, however, that what had changed, was not Emma, but his perception of her, as the veil gradually lifted and he saw her in her true light.

In a poem entitled, ironically, *Side by Side*, the terrible consequences of Hardy's and Emma's ill-fated union becomes apparent when the 'estranged two' meet one day, by chance, at church, and find themselves sharing the same pew.

Thus side by side
Blindly alighted,
They seemed united
As groom and bride,
Who'd not communed
For many years –
Lives from twain spheres
With hearts distuned.

In *Read by Moonlight* he (Hardy) reads the last letter which Emma had written to him, the last of many such 'missives of pain and pine'. In *A Gentleman's Epitaph on Himself and a Lady, Who were Buried Together*, Hardy appears to anticipate his own death and burial next to his late wife. In the poem, he discloses that although the 'Lady' was and would be his companion forever, she was also a person whom he did not really know.

Not a word passed of love all our lifetime,
 Between us, nor thrill;
We'd never a husband-and-wife time,
 For good or for ill.

Nevertheless, the fact that he loved Emma is borne out by the poem *The Woman I Met*, where he declares

Well; your very simplicity made me love you
 Mid such town dross
Till I set not Heaven itself above you,
 Who grew my Cross

And yet

...despite how I sighed for you;
So you tortured me, who fain would have died for you!

Finally, in *Fetching Her*, he is in despair, as he agonizes over whether it might have been better had he not

...pulled this flower
From the craggy nook it knew,
 And set it in an alien bower;
But left it where it grew!

Miss Ellen ('Nellie') E. Titterington

In September 1921, Gertrude Bugler married her third cousin, Ernest Bugler, a farmer from Beaminster. In that year, Nellie Titterington was appointed parlourmaid at Max Gate. Said she

> The conditions of my employment were: hours of work 7 a.m. to 10 p.m., one half-day off during the week, and, in one week, a Sunday morning off, and in the next week, a Sunday afternoon and evening off. My wages were £2 16s. a month, with room and meals. I had to supply my own uniforms.[2]

Years later, Nellie described how

> Gone are the five owls which used to sit on the branches at night

Thomas Hardy and HRH The Prince of Wales at Max Gate, summer 1923.
Photo: The National Trust

outside the pink room window [probably the window of the first study, which later became a bedroom] with their eyes shining like lamps. We often used to fetch Mr Hardy to see them. On first entering the room one had quite a shock to see their reflections through the window, and their hooting noises rather scared one.[3]

What of Hardy's relationship with the household staff at Max Gate? Opinions are mixed. His chauffeur, Harold Voss, said that he never saw Hardy in a temper. He was a 'real gentleman' who was 'never flurried' but always calm.[4] On the other hand, Hardy's gardener, Bertie Stephens, who managed the 1-acre garden, conservatory, greenhouse and paddock single-handed, declared that

> at no time did Hardy express any appreciation or give any praise for anything that was done in the garden. He took everything for granted. [Also] he could also get into a bit of a mood [and be] irritable.[5]

Margaret Male, stated that it was Hardy's manner never to acknowledge his employees if he encountered them in the street. She attributed this to his shyness.[6] Nellie Titterington, said that although Hardy gave the maids at Max Gate

> quiet little smiles as he passed them on the stairs, he never passed the time of day with them, unless it was to talk about the weather.

Fourteen

FINAL YEARS

In May 1922 Hardy visited his former family home at Higher Bockhampton and was distressed to see that both house and garden had become shabby through lack of care.

At Max Gate on 25 June 1922, Siegfried Sassoon declared

> Probably it is sentimentality on my part, but it did seem rather poignant to be playing 'She wore a Wreath of Roses' while T.H. sang the words with most naive simplicity.
>
> Somehow the episode of his singing that old ballad seems infinitely precious. Ridiculous words by the author of 'The Mistletoe Bough'! Yet he sang them with tenderness, as though he were handling some relic of youth long-cherished and hallowed by memory. And he does these things with the same half-humorous seriousness and simplicity that pervade his poems. This quality is the key-note to his greatness. It is his strength and his sweetness. It makes me feel a grateful worm...
>
> People complain that he is over-sensitive to criticism; but the old wounds still rankle; he certainly does worry too much about the small pin-pricks of reviewers. And he has his little vanities about his work; dislikes criticism except when favourable. But, as I've said again and again, he is fundamentally humble.[1]

July 1922 brought another visit from Sassoon, and also visits from Florence Henniker, Edmund Blunden and E. M. Forster. In August Florence said of her eighty-two-year-old husband

> T. H. is really wonderfully well. Yesterday he cycled to Talbothays and did it well, not even feeling tired afterwards.[2]

In November Florence, who was now answering Hardy's letters on his behalf, wrote to Lady Josephine Sackville, who had requested that Hardy autograph some books for her. The answer was that yes, Mr Hardy was prepared to do so, but only on payment of the fee of haif a guinea for each one; the sum of which would be forwarded to the Dorset County Hospital.[3]

The tenth anniversary of Emma's death fell on 27 November 1922, and he and Florence marked the occasion by placing flowers on her tomb and on the tombs of other members of the Hardy family.

May O'Rourke was secretary at Max Gate from 27 March 1923. Said she

When the evening closed in and dinner was over, Mrs Hardy would read aloud to him; the choice ranged from memoirs, history, and biography, and his familiar loves among the English poets, to the latest modern works.

One day we were all out in the garden when he asked me suddenly if I knew a poem about the execution of Mary Queen of Scots, which had been popular in his youth. I did not know it. 'Would you like me to say it to you?' he asked. I agreed warmly, and he stood before me, his hands folded like a child, and recited the numerous verses without hesitation. When he had finished, Hardy looked at me gently and quizzically and he said: 'It's not poetry – it's not poetry! – but it's none the worst for that!'

Although he kept to his daily routine, as the dark winter days closed in his wife, at least, must have had her own disquieted thoughts. One day in December, he seated himself as usual at his writing table, only to find that now his work was beyond him. So the pen was laid aside, where poetry was concerned; he used it finally, to write a splendid signature on a cheque for the Society of Authors, two days before he died.[4]

On 4 April 1923 the death of Florence Henniker brought to an end her thirty-year friendship with Hardy. In her Will, she bequeathed the letters that Hardy had sent to her to his widow, Florence, who on this occasion elected to preserve, rather than destroy them.

In May, Hardy was visited by the poet Walter de la Mare and caricaturist and author Max Beerbohm and his wife Florence. In June the Hardys visited Oxford and stayed two nights at Queen's College (which, in November 1922, had made him an Honorary Fellow), calling on the way at Fawley in Berkshire, where his maternal grandmother had spent the first thirteen years of her life as an orphan.

William Herbert Weston, who worked as gardener at Max Gate for four months in 1923/1924, said of Hardy 'he always paid me far above the [going] rate'.

One of the places in the garden was a sacred spot and nobody was allowed to tidy it up, this was a broken down old garden seat covered with brambles. Mr Hardy used to sit there with his first wife.[5]

On 20 July 1923, Hardy was invited to Dorchester to meet the Prince of Wales (later King Edward VIII), who was there to open a new drill hall for the Dorset Territorial Army, after which the Prince was entertained to luncheon by the Hardys at Max Gate. On that occasion, said Nellie Titterington

> Mr Hardy spoke to the Prince about a piece of land we called The Paddock, that he would like to have for a kitchen garden. I think it was Duchy of Cornwall Estate, because the Prince said he would see about it.

The outcome was that Hardy was granted the extra land.[6] The following month Hardy explained why he objected to 'anything like an interview for press purposes'. It was because he had been the victim of 'so much fabrication and misrepresentation in the past'.[7]

In September 1923 Florence said that Hardy had told her

> he would have welcomed a child when we married first, ten years ago, but now it would kill him with anxiety to have to father one.[8]

The *Famous Tragedy of the Queen of Cornwall*, a poetic, one-act play for mummers, was published by Macmillan on 15 November 1923. Swinburne had already written a romance in couplets on the subject in 1882, but now Hardy himself had brought back to life the legendary tale of Tristram, who falls in love with Queen Iseult of Ireland, but actually marries her namesake, Iseult of Brittany.

In late December 1923, George Bernard Shaw and his wife, Charlotte, visited the Hardys, as did Colonel T. E. Lawrence (of Arabia), who had enlisted earlier that year as a private soldier in the Tank Training School at Bovington under the assumed name of 'T. E. Shaw'. Lawrence lived in a remote cottage called Clouds Hill, which lay 7 miles from Max Gate. Said gardener Bertie Stephens

> Lawrence would arrive on his powerful motorcycle at great speed and brake hard in the drive. [9]

On 7 February 1924 Kate Hardy learnt that Florence had been appointed a Borough Magistrate.[10]

Anniversaries were, as always, important to Hardy, who on 3 April 1924 recorded in his diary: 'Mother died twenty years ago today.'

On 21 April he wrote to General John H. Morgan (lawyer and author, who had been involved in the implementation of the disarmament provisions of the Treaty of Versailles, which marked the end of the Great War). In his letter, Hardy expressed the desire that the League of Nations (which had been inaugurated in January 1920) would offer 'a real hope' that

> principalities & powers will discern more & more clearly that each personality in them stands himself to lose by war.

He thought it wrong to blame the English, either entirely, or mainly, for the current poverty in Ireland, which he believed was caused by 'the temperament' of that country's people – whom he nonetheless considered to be 'romantic & generous'.[11]

In July 1924 players from Balliol College, Oxford, arrived to perform the Greek tragedy *Oresteia* in the garden of Max Gate. In October, said Norrie (Augusta Noreen, sister of Gertrude Bugler) Woodhall

> Thomas Hardy requested that the entire cast [for *Tess of the D'Urbervilles*, to be staged in Dorchester from 26-29 November 1924 by the Hardy Players] should come to Max Gate… to rehearse there. He was then a frail old man, not wanting to go to a dress rehearsal in the Corn Exchange where the Press would be present.

At the end of the rehearsal, said Norrie

> Thomas Hardy beckoned to me to come to the table. He asked for my script, saying, 'I haven't given Liza-Lu much to say, have I?' He seemed to me, then so young, to be a very old man who sensed my acute shyness and love of acting. He added the two words 'Tess, Tess' which was all I had to say after rushing across the stage to throw myself in Tess' arms, [together with] the sentence 'I'm so glad you have come home.' Then he returned my script to me with a twinkle in his eye, saying 'that's better isn't it?'. I thanked him, feeling he, so shy himself, understood me, and was trying to help me.[12]

A member of the Hardy Players (the new name, since 1920, of the Dorchester Debating, Literary and Dramatic Society) was Norman J. Atkins, an employee of a bank in Dorchester, who was to play Alec D'Urberville in the forthcoming production of *Tess*. At Max Gate, said he

> I remember the China tea and the microscopic pieces of bread and butter of lace-like thinness which looked like a collection of pale yellow and brown postage stamps decorating the plate on which they were served…
>
> Mr Hardy helped rearrange the furniture to give us space in which to act and was in one of his best moods; he was an entirely different man, but it was to Tess [Gertrude Bugler] that he directed most of his animated conversation.

In other words, in the presence of a beautiful woman, Hardy had come to life! As for Florence, said Atkins, who he described as being 'slight in stature', she

> usually wore dark plain dresses with little or no jewellery. She had

> a nervous habit of slightly pursing or twisting her lips when speaking, which was particularly noticeable at the beginning of a conversation. Her hair was dark brown, parted at the side and looped into a bun at the back of her head. She used no make-up and had rather a pale complexion. Her expression was very sad at times, almost to the point of misery. Yet behind that sad expression there lurked a real sense of fun.

When Atkins found himself alone with Florence Hardy in the drawing room, he said

> The subject of her conversation took me completely by surprise. While she fully appreciated the acting talents of her husband's 'stage heroine' she was most definitely put out by his obvious appreciation and friendliness towards the lady herself [i.e. Gertrude Bugler]. She was also convinced that this was a matter of some comment amongst the [Hardy] Players themselves and that was most undesirable.[13]

Atkins, however, thought that Florence 'was taking the matter far too seriously'. But of course, she knew Hardy far better than he! Surely it is no coincidence that in Florence Hardy's *The Life of Thomas Hardy*, neither Gertrude Bugler nor the Hardy Players receive a single mention.

Atkins subsequently had another revelation to make. In the 1970s, he told James Gibson, Principal Lecturer at Christ Church College, Canterbury, Kent and editor of *Thomas Hardy: Interviews and Recollections*, that

> Once… his [Atkins'] wife had been informed by a man that half the population were descendants of Hardy's illegitimate children, and that a cousin of his in Cranborne had been told that the 'Fleur de Lys' was the pub where Hardy's girl friend walked into the bar stark naked.[14]

Taken in isolation, this account might easily be dismissed as meaningless gossip. However, in the light of what is known about Hardy's other dalliances, perhaps there is some truth in it after all. For example, evidence has been presented elsewhere by the author that during his time at 'Riverside Villa', Sturminster Newton with Emma – i.e. prior to the Max Gate years – he had fathered an illegitimate daughter by his housemaid.[15]

In late October 1924, Norman Atkins received a visit from Dr Smerdon who was to take the part of Angel Clare, in the forthcoming performance of *Tess*. Smerdon, said Atkins

> had conceived the brilliant idea of arranging a rehearsal that afternoon at Wool Manor (the Wellbridge Manor of the play) and had

obtained the consent of the then occupiers. He had invited Mr and Mrs Hardy, Gertrude Bugler and Harry Tilley [Thomas Henry Tilley, one time Mayor of Dorchester and member of the Hardy Players] to meet there, and he said that he would drive me over with his wife and that we had been invited to tea afterwards at Max Gate.

The rehearsal was only a short one and concerned the tragic 'confession scene' between Tess and Angel Clare on their honeymoon; and the subsequent meeting of Tess with Alec. Here was one of the world's most eminent men of letters in the late evening of his life, watching the heroine, whom he had himself created, come to life in the very house of the scene which he had visualised. Undoubtedly she was the very incarnation of Tess Derbyfield [D'Urberville] of the novel, and as he sat and watched he appeared to be deeply moved.[16]

On 26 November 1924, said Kate Hardy, the first performance of *Tess of the D'Urbervilles* duly 'took place at the Corn Exchange this morning'.[17] Among those present were Florence Hardy, Colonel T. E. Lawrence, E. M. Forster, and Siegfried Sassoon. 'Mr Hardy was not present, but came into the hall afterwards to meet his wife and guests'.[18] Said Norman Atkins

Following the performance... the critics and press reporters from London newspapers were loud in their praises – and justly so.[19]

According to Norrie Woodhall

It was just after 'Tess' was staged in Dorchester that negotiations were in progress regarding my sister Gertrude, playing Tess in London with a professional cast in a series of matinees. Florence Hardy by this time had become insanely jealous of my sister. Apparently she imagined Thomas Hardy was becoming infatuated with her. Perhaps Florence could not understand that the Tess he had created in his mind gave him so much pleasure to be able to see, after all those years since he had created her. Florence was actually driven to Beaminster, unknown to her husband, to beg my sister not to go to London as Tess. All sorts of excuses were made, except the truth, and eventually my poor sister agreed to write the letter of refusal. Thomas Hardy must have thought her to be very ungrateful. He died not knowing the truth.[20]

On 31 December Hardy 'sat up' and heard the chimes of Big Ben on the wireless, heralding the New Year.

Nellie Titterington had an amusing story to tell, of an incident that occurred at about this time.

> Hardy's wireless broke down, and it was fun to see Miss Philpotts and Hardy crawling on the floor testing the wires, to see if they could get it go, Hardy giving her useless advice and laughing like a boy. He was so pleased when she got it to go and told her how clever she was.[21]

The person referred to above was probably (Mary) Adelia (Eden) Phillpotts (born 1896), daughter of Eden Phillpotts and his first wife Emily.

In April 1925, Hardy travelled to Glastonbury in Somerset, for a production of *The Famous Tragedy of the Queen of Cornwall*, a performance at which Vera Mardon and her father were in attendance. In order that his visit be kept a secret, it was arranged for Hardy to occupy a tiny, curtained room at the rear of the hall, facing the stage. After the performance, and believing that the audience had departed, Hardy 'crept out' only to be pounced upon by two enthusiastic American ladies, one of whom thrust out her hand and said 'Gee! Mr Hardy! may I have the honour of shaking you by the hand'. Said Vera

> Hardy was caught in just the situation he always dreaded. He very reluctantly allowed her to shake him momentarily by the hand, quietly muttering 'Oh yes!', then quickly jerked his hand free and rapidly turned on his heels and shot out of the hall to his hired car, at what, even for him, was a remarkably fast pace. He reminded us of a frightened rabbit scurrying back to its burrow.[22]

2 June 1925 was Hardy's birthday. Said Kate Hardy

> Henry and I went to Max Gate to see Tom. We took him a bunch of flowers – descendants of those which were blooming at Bockhampton when he was born. Also some stocks.[23]

Said Harold Voss of Hardy's brother

> When Henry was seventy-three he wanted to learn to drive a car and I taught him. My firm supplied him with an open touring Sunbeam with a Coatleen engine, which I drove down from Wolverhampton for him.
>
> I can never remember Thomas Hardy being driven by his brother Henry, who was a faster driver than I was, and I don't think Hardy felt safe being driven fast.[24]

On 15 July 1925, said Dr Thomas Loveday of Bristol University, 'carrying our robes and one for him', a 'small deputation' arrived at Max Gate with the purpose of awarding Hardy the Honorary Degree of Doctor of Letters.[25] This was the fifth university to honour him in this way.

Hardy was clearly enjoying a social life at Max Gate such as he had never experienced with Emma. 'Would you care to spend Wednesday or Thursday night here?' Florence enquired of Sydney Cockerell in early August 1925. Prior to that, said she

> We have promised to lunch with Dr & Mrs Head at Lyme Regis, on Thursday next, & go on to tea with Lady Pinney at Racedown.[26]

According to Nellie Titterington, 'one older person' that Hardy

> would brighten up for was Lady [Hester] Pinney of Racedown Manor [in the Marshwood Vale, west Dorsetshire], and she would always sit on the hearth rug and talk and talk, and Hardy would laugh out loud and chuckle over bits she told him of the local gossip. One did not often hear Hardy laugh.[27]

Major General Sir Harry R. W. Marriott Smith, of Wareham House, Dorchester, said of Hardy

> What struck me as a soldier was the indomitable courage with which he always refused to blur in any way the ugly facts of the world. The suffering came home to him so nearly and so hardly that he found it difficult to forgive the powers that directed our existence, for the pain and the grief that he saw all around him. He would not accept my own view that the suffering of others could be exaggerated – that there was a limit to human suffering, and that we did not, could not expect to know the whole of the plan of the universe. 'No,' he said 'we've got to face it, we are up against a power which may be indifferent, may be malignant and is extremely unlikely to be benevolent.'[28]

On a more personal note, poet, critic, biographer and astrologer Martin Seymour-Smith stated that Hardy

> at the age of eighty-five, told Edmund Blunden – and Blunden himself said it to this author as he did to others – that 'sexual desire could be a great problem for an old man'. He then mentioned that he had been capable of full sexual intercourse until he was eighty-four.[29]

Surely this is confirmation a), that Hardy had enjoyed a full sexual relationship with Florence and b), that his dislike of being physically touched did not preclude this.

On 28 September 1925, said Kate Hardy, Hardy and Florence called in at Talbothays at 4 p.m.

> for a few minutes on their way back from the heath. They had been to get some fern for storing apples.[30]

(Dried fern was found to be ideal for the preservation of apples, which were laid on it and then covered with it.) The evening of 6 December 1925 was a memorable one, said Nellie Titterington

> when the Philip Ridgeway Company played 'Tess' to Mr and Mrs Hardy in the drawing room at Max Gate. They came from [the Garrick Theatre] London, and Miss Gwen Ffrangcon Davies played Tess. Max Gate became alive that evening for the players were everywhere and it certainly made the 'Hardy' night.[31]

Meanwhile, Hardy's *Human Shows, Far Phantasies, Songs, and Trifles* was published on 20 November 1925 by Macmillan. The poems contain a medley of favourite themes: *The Turnip Hoer, The Monument Maker, A Sheep Fair, The Graveyard of Dead Creeds,* and so forth; the majority of them revealing Hardy in a lighter mood than heretofore. However, Emma is never far from his thoughts, as for instance in *Last Love-Word,* which ends with the couplet:

> When that first look and touch,
> Love, doomed us two!

In *A Second Attempt* he describes how:

> Thirty years after
> I began again
> An old-time passion:
> And it seemed as fresh as when
> The first day ventured on:
> When mutely I would waft her
> In Love's past fashion
> Dreams much dwelt upon
> Dreams I wished she knew.

This poem was written, according to the original manuscript, in 'about 1900' – four years before he first met Florence Dugdale. So did Hardy actually make another attempt to woo Emma, who he had first met thirty years previously in March 1870? Whatever the truth may be, however, his 'hot hopes' that the relationship would progress to 'consummation' proved to be in vain, for 'Twice-over cannot be!'

In his poem *A Poor Man and a Lady,* Hardy's feelings of inferiority surface once again, when, after a period of 'timorous secret bliss', the couple become 'divided'. '...never a kiss/Of mine could touch you', says Hardy, whose marriage to 'a comely woman of noble kith' was therefore 'not a valid thing'

– i.e. because it was loveless on her part. Other poems, such as *Known Had I*, *Her Haunting-Ground* and *Days to Recollect*, also reflect his regret for lost or absent love.

On 23 December 1925 Hardy remembered and recorded in his diary the tenth anniversary of his beloved sister Mary's death.

> She came into the world... and went out... and the world is just the same... not a ripple on the surface left.[32]

This was not strictly true, for apart from anything else, Mary left for posterity some fine portraits which she had painted in oils of members of her family, without which our knowledge of them would have been that much the poorer.

On 25 December Florence recalled a previous Christmas Day, that of 1910:

> when I sat here [at Max Gate] alone, & vowed that no power on earth would ever induce me to ever spend another Christmas Day at Max Gate. T. H. had gone off to Bockhampton to see his sisters, after a violent quarrel with the first Mrs T. H. because he wanted me to go to see the sisters too, & she said I shouldn't because they would poison my mind against her.[33]

In the course of that year, 1925, more than one hundred people had signed Max Gate's visitors book.

In January 1926 Hardy relinquished his governorship of Dorchester Grammar School. Sitting on committees, which 'controlled or ordained the activities of others', had never been his favourite pastime. Instead, he preferred to be 'the man with the watching eye' – in other words, simply an observer of events.[34]

Hardy's letter-writing continued unabated, albeit with the help of Florence, upon whom he was increasingly reliant in this respect due to his failing eyesight. Among those with whom he corresponded in 1926 were J. B. Priestley, H. G. Wells, John Galsworthy and Gustav Holst. He also wrote to Marie Stopes (the Scottish pioneer campaigner for birth-control); in fact, it was characteristic of him to associate with avant-garde women. February found him entering into correspondence regarding the condition of the bells of Stinsford church, which had fallen into disrepair.[35]

In March 1926 Hardy's sister, Kate, accompanied Florence to a matinee performance by the *Tess* touring company at Bournemouth. However, Hardy himself 'did not feel equal' to the outing.[36]

In his poem *He Never Expected Much*, Hardy reflected on his eighty-sixth birthday, which he had celebrated on 2 June. The poem begins

Well, World, you have kept faith with me,
  Kept faith with me;
Upon the whole you have proved to be
  Much as you said you were.
Since as a child I used to lie
Upon the leaze and watch the sky,
Never, I own, expected I
  That life would all be fair.

The second verse of the poem ends

Many have loved me desperately,
Many with smooth serenity,
While some have shown contempt of me
  Till they dropped underground.

Of those alluded to in this latter couplet, Hardy would undoubtedly have included Emma. The poem ends with a voice seeming to speak to Hardy which is reminiscent of that of his mother, Jemima, when she warned him about the

> figure [which] stands in our path with arm uplifted, to knock us back from any pleasant prospect we indulge in.

"I do not promise overmuch,
  Child; overmuch;
Just neutral-tinted haps and such,"
  You said to minds like mine.
Wise warning for your credit's sake!
Which I for one failed not to take,
And hence could stem such strain and ache
  As each year might assign.

In July 1926 Hardy, in a letter to Edward Clodd, voiced his fear that 'rational religion does not make much [head] way at present'. In fact, the 'movement of thought' appeared to have 'entered a back current in the opposite direction', which was however 'not uncommon in human history'.[37]

Two months later he received an ovation at the William Barnes Theatre in Weymouth, where he was attending a dramatization of *The Mayor of Casterbridge*. In November, with Florence, he made what was to be his last visit to the old family home at Higher Bockhampton. That same month T. E. Lawrence, of whom Hardy was immensely fond, set out for a new RAF

The Barnes Theatre Players perform Tess for Hardy in the drawing room at Max Gate, 1924. Photo: The National Trust

posting in India.

At about this time, Wessex fell ill. Said Nellie Titterington

> an eiderdown was fetched and Wessie was wrapped in it and laid by the dining room fire, with the Hardys and all of us in attendance from time to time, but we could all see Wessie was dying. Rather than disturb him Hardy suggested all meals should be taken to the drawing room.[38]

Lady Grove's death on 7 December 1926 inevitably evoked a poem from Hardy the title of which was *Concerning Agnes.*

> I am stopped from hoping what I have hoped before -
> Yes, many a time! -
> To dance with that fair woman yet once more
> As in the prime
> Of August, when the wide-faced moon looked through
> The boughs at the faery lamps of the Larmer Avenue.

And the second verse begins

I could not, though I should wish, have over again
That old romance,
And sit apart in the shade as we sat then
After the dance
The while I held her hand, and, to the booms
Of contrabassos, feet still pulsed from the distant rooms.

Carol singers arrived at Max Gate at Christmas, as was traditional, this time from St Peter's church, Dorchester. On 27 December, the 'devoted and masterful' dog Wessex died. Said gardener Bertie Stephens

> it was my task to bury him in the animals' graveyard at Max Gate. By the time I buried him there were already some 12 or 13 dogs and cats there, each with its own tombstone.[39]

Hardy designed Wessex's headstone himself. It was inscribed with the words

The Famous Dog
WESSEX
August 1913 - 27 Dec. 1926
Faithful. Unflinching.

Hardy also commemorated his canine friend and companion for thirteen years with a poem, in which Wessex, in his after life, is searching in vain for his master. On New Year's Eve Hardy did not 'sit up' to see the New Year in.

On 2 June 1927 Hardy celebrated his eighty-seventh birthday not at home, but in Devonshire in the company of his friends, actor, producer, dramatist and critic Harley Granville Barker and his wife Helen.

On 21 July, accompanied by Florence, Hardy laid the commemoration stone of Hardye's School, Dorchester's newly-built grammar school for boys. This event would have given one such as he, who cherished education and learning, great pleasure. The school had been founded in 1569 by Thomas Hardye (sometimes spelt Hardy) of Melcombe Regis and Frampton, to give local pupils a free education. To mark the event, said Nellie Titterington, he was presented with

> a silver trowel in a case and it had the place of honour on a round table in the drawing room. He was a proud man that day.[40]

On 6 August 1927, composer Gustav Holst was granted permission by Hardy to dedicate his orchestral composition entitled *Egdon Heath* to the latter. Three days later, Hardy paid a special visit to the eponymous heath, and also to Puddletown church, where his ancestors had been members of the choir ('quire').[41] This month and the following one brought visits to Bath, Ilminster and Yeovil, Lulworth Castle and Charborough Park.

John C. Squire, writer and editor of the *London Mercury,* visited Max Gate on several occasions the last being on 24 August 1927.

> My own last glimpse of him I shall always especially cherish as it was the best, leaving a picture which embodies the very essence of Hardy the English countryman and Hardy the unexhausted old man. Knowing it would give him pleasure, I brought with me a splendid and celebrated singer of sea-shanties and traditional songs – Mr John Goss. From lunch till tea we had music. First there were Dorset folk-songs. The old man took great delight in supplying alternative versions remembered from his youth, and whenever there was a refrain Hardy's light but vigorous old voice joined in, whilst his hand beat the air to the time. 'Well, well, well!' he chuckled, tears of pleasure in his eyes as each old favourite appeared. One thing led to another; long-neglected music books of the mid-Victorian age were sent for; we carolled 'The Mocking-Bird' and other such sentimental ditties. I thought of all the poems he had made on such themes… He was steeped in the social history of England and of his countryside.[42]

US novelist Ellen Glasgow visited Max Gate on 2 September 1927, when Hardy

> told me he missed Wessex more and more. 'Wessex was so fond of the wireless', he said, 'that I used to get up early in the morning and come down stairs and turn it on for him.' And presently he took me out into the garden, and showed me the little grave where Wessex was buried.[43]

In the first week of October 1927, Harold Voss drove Hardy to Ilminster in Somerset 'to see something (a tomb I think) in the church'.[44]

In late October 1927 Hardy and Florence took a short stroll from Max Gate across the fields. However, from now on he would be taken everywhere by motor car; for example, to Stinsford, to put flowers on the family graves, and to Talbothays to see his siblings, Henry and Kate. In that year, in excess of one hundred people had signed Max Gate's visitors book.[45]

On Armistice Day, 11 November 1927, the ninth anniversary of the end of the Great War, Hardy and Florence listened to the Service of Thanksgiving broadcast on the wireless from Canterbury Cathedral.[46]

Thursday 24 November and Sunday 27 November marked the anniversaries of the deaths of his sister Mary and wife Emma respectively. On the latter occasion, Hardy wore a black hat and carried Emma's black walking stick as tokens of his mourning.

Over the years it had been Hardy's habit to sit at his writing-table every morning at 10 a.m. If the spirit moved him, he would write; if it did not, he would find something else to do. This was a ritual which he always observed. On 11 December 1927, however, he was unable to work. On Christmas Day he wrote to (now 'Sir') Edmund Gosse.

> I am in bed on my back, living on butter-broth & beef tea, the servants being much concerned at my not being able to eat any Christmas pudding.[47]

Dr Edward W. Mann takes up the story.

> I was the Hardy family doctor for several years prior to his death in January 1928. He was seldom ill and required very little medical attention until just before Christmas 1927, when he caught a chill and was confined to bed. At first his illness seemed to run a normal course, except for the extreme weakness which I suppose one might expect in a person over eighty. After a couple of weeks, as he didn't seem to be gaining strength, a medical specialist from Bournemouth was called [i.e. the distinguished neurologist Sir Henry Head] in consultation. For a short time Hardy seemed to improve a little...[48]

This was a severe winter and snow lay deep on the ground. As the evening of 11 January 1928 drew in, Hardy asked Florence to read him a verse from the *Rubaiyat* of Omar Khayyam.

Oh, Thou, who Man of baser Earth did'st make,
And who with Eden did'st devise the Snake;
For at the Sin wherewith the Face of Man
Is blacken'd – Man's forgiveness give – and take!

In this, Hardy demonstrated that his relationship with the 'Creator' must of necessity be a two-way process – a 'trade off' – whereby the latter must forgive Hardy his sins, in return for which Hardy would do likewise for his Creator.

Meanwhile, Scottish playwright and novelist and Hardy's 'friend of many years', J. M. Barrie,[49] arrived from London with offers of help. Incidentally, both Hardy and Barrie were members of London's Omar Khayyam Club, which had been founded in 1892 to celebrate both the eponymous poem, and also the poet and scholar Edward Fitzgerald, who had translated it into English.

Continued Dr Mann

On January 11th I was paying my usual evening visit and sitting in his bedroom with his wife, Florence Hardy, and her sister, Miss [Eva] Dugdale – she was a trained nurse – he was telling me about a book called *Possible Worlds* by J. B. S. Haldane, which he was reading, but found too deep! Then all four of us were talking rather light-heartedly about how we would celebrate when the patient was able to get up and come downstairs, when suddenly there was a short sharp cry as Hardy complained of acute pain in his chest, and in spite of everything that we could do, he became more and more breathless and after two or three minutes, he passed on.[50]

The time was shortly after 9 p.m. Said Nellie Titterington

I often think… about the evening of Mr Hardy's death; - Mrs Hardy, Miss Eva Dugdale [Florence's sister], and Sir Sidney Cockerell downstairs at dinner, myself taking watch for Miss Eva.

As Nellie and the other maids sat

just waiting sitting on a large fender by the kitchen fire, wondering [Cockerell came] to tell us Mr Hardy had passed away, and that he had various messages to send, and I am sure it was he who got in touch with the B.B.C. for it to be announced on the 9 p.m. News. Mr Cockerell had been staying in the house for some days. Mrs Hardy had told him of Mr Hardy's illness.

Whereupon Nellie offered to cycle immediately to Talbothays to inform Hardy's sister Kate, but Florence said

no, Mr Hardy would not like you cycling out so late at night… so I cycled over to Talbothays next morning to tell her.[51]

Fifteen

AFTERMATH

Said Dr Mann

> On the next and following days there was great discussion as to where the burial should take place. His widow felt as he belonged so much to Dorset, the funeral should be in Stinsford, the family burying ground, but Sir James Barrie, a great friend of the family thought it ought to be in Westminster Abbey. Finally, the Vicar of Stinsford suggested that the heart should be removed for burial in the family grave and the remains cremated for burial in the Abbey. This was agreed to by the widow and when the necessary permission was obtained, my partner and I removed the heart and placed it in a casket for burial in Stinsford, and later the remains were taken to Woking for cremation.[1]

Hardy's sister Kate was not at all pleased. Said she

> It seems they want to bury Tom at Westminster Abbey – it seems the wish of Mr Cockerell, Sir James Barrie & Florence. H [Henry] & I prefer Stinsford of course as we understand he wished to lie there but they say that among his papers is a notice to the effect that 'if the nation desires it otherwise' he can be buried at Westminster Ch [i.e. Abbey].

Also, for Kate, the fact that 'Tom is to be cremated' was yet 'another staggering blow'.[2]

Hardy's cousin Theresa was of the same opinion, she having previously told a reporter from the press

> I am grieved that they are going to take poor Tom away to London. He wanted I know, 'to lie with his own folk in the [Stinsford] churchyard'. But it was not to be.[3]

Hardy's ashes were nonetheless duly interred in Westminster Abbey in Poets' Corner at 2 p.m. on Monday 16 January 1928; a spadeful of his beloved Dorsetshire soil having been sprinkled on the casket. The last novelist to be buried there prior to this was Charles Dickens in 1870. Hardy had never been introduced to Dickens, a fellow champion of the poor and underprivileged, although he had attended some of his readings at the Hanover Square Rooms in London in the 1860s.[4]

Hardy's pallbearers were Conservative prime minister, Stanley Baldwin; leader of the opposition, Ramsay MacDonald; Sir James Barrie, John Galsworthy, Sir Edmund Gosse, A. E. Housman, Rudyard Kipling and George Bernard Shaw. Others present included Hardy's widow Florence; his sister Kate; the heads of Magdalene College, Cambridge, and Queen's College, Oxford, and members of the Macmillan publishing house.

On 16 January 1928, referring to the funeral, Kate declared

> it was all very very mournful & hopeless & strange & I was relieved when it was over.[5]

Meanwhile, at Stinsford's church of St Michael, Hardy's heart was buried in the tomb of his first wife Emma. Adjacent to this tomb is, on the one side, that of his sister Mary, and on the other that of his parents, Thomas II and Jemima. Beyond are buried his grandfather, Thomas I; his grandmother, Mary; his uncle, James, and finally, his aunt, Jane, and his cousin, Theresa.

Said Nellie Titterington, Hardy's trustees

> paid £2 10s. for black coats for the servants to attend his funeral [the so-called 'heart-funeral']. This had been a wish expressed by Hardy before he died, and was much appreciated by the staff.[6]

Then came a startling revelation from Nellie. 'Until the funeral Mrs Hardy had kept Mr Hardy's heart in my biscuit tin'. Said Norman Atkins,

> the casket [i.e. tin] was accepted by his cook [and] placed on the sideboard in the dining room, the door being locked for safe keeping.[7]

Continued Nellie

> At his funeral, sitting in the seats in front of us maids, were some Dorset gentry in their hunting kit. This would have upset Mr Hardy very much indeed, as he was bitterly opposed to what he considered the cruelty of hunting, indeed, he was very sensitive to every form of cruelty. He was a man of very great compassion.[8]

Bertie Stephens remembered that day vividly.

> The hearse for the removal of the heart-casket arrived at about 7.55 a.m., and as it was driven up the drive towards the porch this horde of pressmen and photographers began to follow, and in accordance with Mrs Hardy's instructions I intercepted them and asked them please to return to the road.
>
> A few minutes after eight Mr Hannah, the head undertaker of Hannah and Hollands, brought from the house a handful of narcissi,

one of Hardy's favourite flowers, and strewed them over the floor of the hearse. At about ten minutes past eight the heart-casket was carried by the bearers towards the hearse followed by Mrs Hardy... and then the funeral procession wended its way to Stinsford church for the ceremony. The church was packed to the doors, and both sides of the road and path outside the church were crowded with people. The townspeople of Dorchester were well represented.[9]

Having returned home by train, Kate confirmed that Stinsford's

Church & Churchyard were packed. H [Henry] threw some violets on the casket according to his own wish.[10]

Meanwhile, a memorial service to Hardy was held in Dorchester's church of St Peter, in the presence of the mayor and corporation and many distinguished dignitaries.

Subsequently, at Max Gate, said Stephens, Florence Hardy

herself burnt... baskets full of the letters and private papers that I had carried down from the study to the garden under her supervision and watchful eye. She would not let me burn these, but insisted upon doing it herself, and after all the papers had been destroyed, she raked the ashes to be sure that not a single scrap or word remained. It was a devil of a clear out. I never knew so much stuff come out of a room or such a burn up.

Whether she was destroying them on her own initiative or carrying out the wishes of her late husband I never knew, and the world will never learn what went up in flames on that 'bonfire day'.[11]

It might be argued that instead of destroying the Hardy archive, Florence ought to have offered it to some learned organization such as a university. However, in failing to do so, a), she may simply have been fulfilling her late husband's wishes, and b), she was simply carrying on with a process which Hardy himself had already begun – viz, his note to himself in his personal notebook, under the heading 'Things Done'

Go through E's papers again [and presumably discard anything incriminatory]. Continue to examine & destroy useless old MSS, entries in note books, & marks [jottings] in printed books.[12]

The estate of Thomas Hardy, the man who removed surplus lumps of coal from the fire if he considered the quantity used by the maid to be extravagant, and who rarely gave a tip, was valued at the colossal sum of £95,418 3s. 1d. In his Will, he had stated as follows. 'It is my wish that I may be buried in Stinsford Churchyard…' In other words, his cremation, the removal of his heart, and the interment of his ashes at Westminster Abbey were all performed contrary to what he had desired for his remains.

Hardy left Max Gate's contents to Florence together with an annuity of £600 to be reduced to £300 should she remarry; royalties from the sale of his books; and Max Gate in trust for her lifetime. There were also small bequests to his cousin John Antell of Puddletown, to his second cousin Charles Meech Hardy of Puddletown, and to his late wife's nephew and niece Gordon Gifford and his sister Lilian repectively. He also left legacies for animal welfare. Surprisingly, he left no bequest to Dorchester Hospital.

Hardy also requested that his literary executors

> cause to be erected in the Church of St Juliot near Boscastle, Cornwall a Tablet memorising my connection with the restoration of the said Church a design for which tablet will be found among my papers.[13]

Hardy had designed a sundial for Max Gate, which he was never to see completed. Manufactured by local iron founders, it was inscribed with the Latin words 'QUID DE NOCTE' –'What of the Night?' – a reference to *Psalm 30*

> Weeping may endure for a night,
> But joy cometh in the morning.

Florence now had the sundial placed on the exteririor wall of the east tower of the house. She now took a flat in Adelphi Terrace, London, and invited Nellie Titterington to

> return and work for her again. Everything was locked up at 'Max Gate'.[14]

However, she continued to employ the gardener, Stephens, who

> stayed on [at Max Gate] for some months after that unhappy event as caretaker.

Florence now set about ensuring that an 'edited version' of Hardy's memory would be preserved for posterity. In early February 1928 she told Sir Edmund Gosse that

> With regard to the biography of my husband I have for many years been collecting material which has been put somewhat roughly into shape. T. H. allowed me to take a great many extracts from his diaries & note books, & supplied all the information that I required.[15]

On 27 February 1928 at Cheltenham, Gustav Holst in person conducted the Birmingham Symphony Orchestra in the premier performance of *Egdon Heath*, his tribute to Hardy. On 5 March, Florence wrote to T. E. Lawrence, thanking him for his kind letters to her and saying

> besides my loneliness, which will never be less, I have to suffer remorse, almost beyond expression, because I know I failed him at every turn. Time will not help me for I know my own nature, and I shall miss him more and more. The thought of years that may have to be lived through without him fills me with terror. There was really nothing in my life except T. H. nor will there ever be.[16]

As time went by, Florence spent less and less time in London and more and more at Max Gate, where she allowed herself some luxuries. Said Stephens

> With the passing of her husband, Mrs Hardy now held the reins, and she soon bought a brand new Austin 14 saloon motor-car, and employed Mr Dick Shipton as her chauffeur. A [new] bathroom was installed in Max Gate itself for Mrs Hardy and her guests. Drains were laid and money was well spent on other much needed improvements.[17]

Published by Macmillan in October 1928, nine months after Hardy's death, the collection of poems entided *Winter Words* contained yet more thinly disguised references to Emma. In *To Louisa in the Lane*, Hardy declares, 'Wait, must I, till with flung-off flesh I follow you', but in *Song to Aurore* he issues a caveat.

We'll not begin again to love
 It only leads to pain...

And in *The Destined Pair* he ponders on whether 'Fate' would 'have been kinder... Had he failed to find her' (i.e. had he never met Emma in the first place).

An outsider, who was unfamiliar with the circumstances of Hardy's marriage to Emma, might miss altogether the possible relevance of another poem in his *Winter Words* collection.

Henley Regatta

She looks from the window: still it pours down direly,
And the avenue drips. She cannot go, she fears;

And the Regatta will be spoilt entirely;
  And she sheds half-crazed tears.
Regatta Day and rain come on together
Again, years after. Gutters trickle loud;
But Nancy cares not. She knows nought of weather,
  Or of the Henley crowd:

She's a Regatta, quite her own. Inanely
She laughs in the asylum as she floats
Within a water-tub, which she calls 'Henley',
  Her little paper boats.

Imagine for a moment that Hardy and Emma are in London for the season, as had been their custom, and that they have decided to attend the Henley Royal Regatta – traditionally held at Henley-on-Thames, Oxfordshire. It is raining, and Emma ('Nancy') therefore declines to attend. Years later, perhaps at the time when the regatta is being held, Emma behaves childishly and makes some paper boats. By this time she has become so deluded that she believes the Henley Regatta is taking place in her bath, in which she is floating her home-made boats. In other words, she has created her own personal 'asylum'.

During June 1928, Dr Mann, made frequent visits to Talbothays to attend Henry, who was ailing.[18] 1 July 1928 marked the latter's seventy-seventh birthday.

On 31 July 1928 Florence told Kate that she was about to depart for London 'for an operation on Friday'.[19] (Florence had several operations on her ears, nose and throat.)

On 9 December 1928, said Kate

> This morning… at 5 a.m. Henry very quietly spread his wings & went to join the 'friends beyond'.

And on the following day

> now life without Henry – how lonely sad & distressful![20]

Henry was buried at Stinsford, in the same tomb as his sister Mary. In his Will, he bequeathed to his sister Kate the portraits in oil by their deceased sister Mary Hardy of their father and mother, of his brother Thomas, and of Florence Hardy for her lifetime, and thereafter to the Trustees of the Dorset County Museum. His house Talbothays, together with nine cottages and land adjoining, he also bequeathed to his sister Kate. Ten cottages in the parish of West Knighton and three cottages, a brickyard, and four acres of land in the parish of Broadmayne he instructed to be sold and the net proceeds to be paid to Kate.[21]

To his brother Thomas (who had, of course, predeceased him), he had bequeathed 'a legacy of Five pounds and my Gold watch as a token of good feeling, more being [considered] unnecessary'. In other words, Henry had adjudged Hardy to be 'well off' and therefore in no need of financial or other support.

On 11 July 1929 Florence wrote to Siegfried Sassoon to say

> I do not think I shall take a house in London, or make any change in my life. I feel that I belong to Max Gate where I can visit Stinsford & go to see my husband's sister [Kate] every few days.[22]

In that year, said Norrie Woodhall, in repect of Gertrude Bugler

> Florence Hardy's conscience must have pricked her very much indeed, for she arranged that my sister should play Tess in London but with another producer who got in touch with my sister to suggest she played Tess at the Duke of York's Theatre. This time she did go to London and was very successful, billed as Hardy's Tess [opening night, 23 July]. It was to be my second visit to London, to stay with my sister for a weekend. She did not like touring afterwards and eventually returned to her home at Beaminster.[23]

On 9 August 1929, said Kate

> Mr Dugdale came after tea followed by F [Florence] in the car. They want me to go to Boscastle with them tomorrow morning and so I am going.[24]

Whilst in Cornwall, on 28 September 1929, Florence and Kate paid a visit to St Juliot, 'to the great pleasure of the solitary little clergyman who lives there'. This was the Reverend David Rhys Morris, who entertained them to tea. However, despite the 'atmosphere of romance', Florence found the experience 'all very sad'.[25] As for Kate, she declared

> I shall never forget that little romantic spot – St Juliot – quite hidden from the rest of the world.[26]

During the summer of 1930, Florence and Kate made several long journeys by car (with Voss at the wheel) including to Topsham, where his late cousin Tryphena Gale (née Sparks) and her sister Rebecca had once lived, and to Dartmoor. Excursions were also made to such places as Salisbury, Lyme Regis, and Torquay, and even as far as the Lake District and Gretna Green.[27]

On 21 November 1930, at a ceremony attended by Kate, a memorial window was unveiled at Stinsford church in memory of Thomas Hardy O.M.[28]

On 10 January 1931 Florence declared that

> with regard to the letters written by T. H. to E. L. G. – afterwards E. L. H. [Emma] – it was *she* who burnt his letters, & he told me he much regretted that at the time, & since. She asked him for her letters to him which he had carefully preserved, & she burnt those too.[29]

On 16 April 1931, within a stone's throw of the former Hardy family home at Bockhampton, a memorial to Hardy was unveiled with Kate in attendance. This was by courtesy of his admirers in the USA. On the same day, she had lunch and tea at Max Gate with Florence. Three days later, she and Florence went to view the memorial together.[30]

On 2 September 1931 Kate attended the unveiling by J. M. Barrie of a bronze statue of Hardy at 'Top-o'-Town', Dorchester by sculptor and painter Eric Henri Kennington.[31]

In May 1932, William Lyon Phelps paid another visit to Max Gate, in company with his wife Annabel. On that occasion, Florence informed him that although her late husband Hardy

> was wholly English and wrote almost exclusively on English themes and of English people, he had the deepest conviction of the brotherhood of mankind, and lived consistently in harmony with this creed. [For example] During the war there was a large German prison-camp near Dorchester; the prisoners were assigned to various tasks in the neighbourhood. Mr Hardy took an interest in every German prisoner who worked on his place. He gave food and medicines, treating them not only with solicitude for their welfare but with respect for them as individuals. Now no one was more eager than Mr Hardy for England's triumph in the war. But his clear intelligence was never clouded by prejudice, and his heart was too big and tender not to be touched by human suffering. It is pleasant to know that these Germans were grateful, that they wrote to their families in Germany about him, and that a letter came back saying that as a result of his consideration, the English prisoners in that part of Germany were receiving better treatment.[32]

On 19 May 1935, T. E. Lawrence died tragically and prematurely. On 21 May, Florence attended his funeral at Moreton.[33] An effigy of Lawrence, also by Eric Kennington and this time carved in Portland stone, was placed in the church of St Martin's-on-the Walls, Wareham, so Hardy and Lawrence, two great friends in life, remain forever, in a sense, united in death.

On 20 January 1936 Kate recorded that King George V had died at 11.55 p.m.[34] On 22 March, said Kate

> I returned some books with Tom's name in them, to Florence & I gave her Tom's ornament of a little house which he had when he was about three years old.[35]

On 24 January 1937, said Kate, 'Miss [i.e. Mrs] Gertrude Bugler called this afternoon'.[36] That spring 1937, Florence was diagnosed with cancer of the bowel for which she went to London in mid May for surgery. However, the cancer was deemed to be inoperable. J. M. Barrie called to see her during her convalescence in a nursing home at Fitzroy Square. This was only a day or two before his own death, on 19 June.[37] She

> spent the last months of her life at Max Gate, always ill and in pain but supported by her sister Margaret and by professional nurses.[38]

Florence died on 15 October 1937 from an illness, which in her own words, she had 'been fighting against for some time…'.[39] She was buried in Stinsford churchyard in the tomb which contained Hardy's heart and the remains of his first wife, Emma. Her Will stipulated that she was to be cremated and that her

> ashes be placed in the grave at Stinsford Churchyard in which my husband's heart is buried and I desire that the inscription which my husband composed with my name and the necessary particulars be placed on the south side of the tomb.

There were also bequests to the Vicar and Churchwardens of the Parish of Stinsford

> to invest the same and to apply the yearly income thereof in keeping the churchyard and particularly the grave of my husband in good order…

As for Max Gate, the house and grounds were to be 'vested in my Trustees upon trust', as were the contents. However Irene Cooper Willis, barrister-at-law and co-executor with Lloyds Bank of the Hardy estate, was tasked with selecting 'such articles, manuscripts, books and letters' as she saw fit to be 'deposited and placed on exhibition' at the Dorset County Museum.

Florence left legacies to her four sisters, to Dorset County Hospital, to Dorchester Grammar School, and to a nephew and two nieces. A property which she owned, 'Egdon', 128 Monmouth Road, Dorchester, she left to her sister Margaret Alicia Soundy.[40]

The sale of Max Gate's contents took place on Wednesday 16 February

1938 at 2 p.m. However, in accordance with Hardy's wishes, the entire contents of his third and final study were left to the Dorset County Museum, where it was painstakingly reconstructed. This included furniture, papers, writing instruments, bookcases containing many first editions and reference books.

The sale of Max Gate itself took place on Friday 6 May 1938. In the event, it was Hardy's sister Kate who purchased the property (even though she continued to live at Talbothays).

On 10 May 1939, Kate noted in her diary

> Opening of the Hardy Memorial Room at Dorchester Museum by John Masefield K.H. cutting the Ribbon.[41]

Kate died on 4 October 1940. She was buried at Stinsford, in the same tomb as her sister Mary and brother Henry. In respect of Max Gate, her will read as follows.

> I Give and Devise the freehold House and garden known as "Max Gate" Dorchester aforesaid which formed the residence of my late brother Thomas Hardy unto The National Trust for Places of Historic Interest or Natural Beauty of No. 7 Buckingham Palace Gardens, London Upon Trust to retain the same in its present condition so far as possible and to use the income thereof for its maintenance and so far as they are able to do so *for the preservation and protection of the house at Higher Bockhampton Stinsford Dorset in which my said brother and I were born in order that so far as practicable the same may be preserved for all time in the same condition as at present* and so far as the income may not be required for those purposes then to apply the balance of the income for the general purposes of the Trust.

Also, Kate bequeathed No. 12 Wollaston Road, Dorchester to Amy Prince her former housekeeper at Talbothays; No. 3 Durngate Street, Dorchester to Harold Voss; her cottage at West Knighton she left to its current incumbent, her gardener John Chutter. There were also bequests to Nathaniel Sparks; Henry Osmond Lock, Hardy's solicitor; Edward Mann, the family doctor; members of the Antell family, and the Rector and Churchwardens of Stinsford. Finally, she bequeathed Talbothays Lodge, and Talbothays Cottages and bungalow to Henry Osmond Lock.[42]

Thomas Hardy
Family Tree

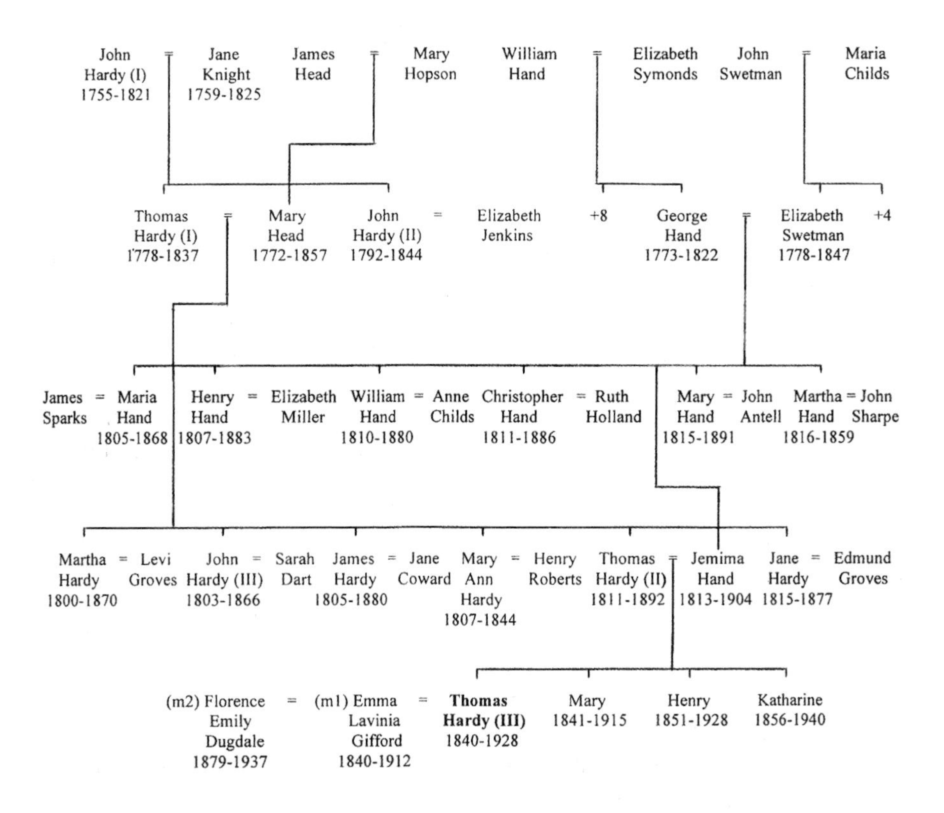

NOTES

Foreword

1. Millgate, Michael (editor), *Letters of Emma and Florence Hardy*, Florence Hardy to Howard Bliss, 10 January 1931.
2. Before destroying Emma's diaries after her death, Hardy first read them aloud to his second wife, Florence.
3. Cox, J. Stevens, (general editor): *Monographs on the Life of Thomas Hardy*, Monograph 6, 'Thomas Hardy in his Garden' by Bertie Norman Stephens, 1963. Bertie Stevens, gardener at Max Gate, described how 'Mrs [Florence] Hardy herself burnt... baskets full of the letters and private papers that I had carried down from the study. It was a devil of a clear out. I never knew so much stuff come out of a room or such a burn up. My impression was she did not want any of the letters or papers to be seen by anyone and she was very careful to destroy every one of them.'
4. Florence Henniker, for example.
5. Millgate, Michael, op. cit., Introducton, p.ix.
6. Millgate, Michael and Richard Little Purdy (editors), *The Collected Letters of Thomas Hardy*, Volume 2, Thomas Hardy to Edward Clodd, 1 April 1894.

2. Max Gate: Beginnings

1. Hardy, Florence Emily, *The Life of Thomas Hardy*, p.166.
2. Ibid, p.171.
3. Hamlin, Garland, *Afternoon Neighbours*. Garland, visited Max Gate on 16 August 1923.
4. F. Stevenson to D. Norton Williams, October-November 1885 (Yale).
5. Hardy, Florence Emily, op. cit., p.176.
6. Ibid, p.176.
7. Ibid, p.201.
8. Information kindly supplied by James Coffey, Honours and Appointments Secretariat, London.
9. Hardy, Florence Emily, op. cit., p.209.
10. Ibid, p.210.
11, Agatha Thornycroft to Hamo Thornycroft, Hamo Thornycroft Archive, Henry Moore Institute, Leeds.
12. Hardy, Florence Emily, op. cit., p.220.
13. Millgate, Michael, *Thomas Hardy: A Biography Revisited*, p.275. A. Thornycroft to H. Thornycroft, 3 July 1889, Mrs E. Manning, *Career*, pp.401-2.
14. Taylor, Richard H. (editor), *The Personal Notebooks of Thomas Hardy*, p.231.
15. Millgate, Michael and Richard Little Purdy (editors), *The Collected Letters of*

Thomas Hardy, Volume 7, Thomas Hardy to Lady Pinney, 20 January 1926.
16. Hardy, Florence Emily, op. cit., p.224.
17. Millgate, Michael and Richard Little Purdy, op. cit., Volume 1, Thomas Hardy to Thackeray Turner, 16 December 1889.
18. Ibid, Thomas Hardy to Lord Lytton, 15 July 1891.
19. Stewart, J. I. M., *Thomas Hardy: A Critical Biography*, p.150.
20. Hardy, Florence Emily, op. cit., pp.226-7.
21. Ibid, p.237.
22. Helier, Lady St, *Memories of Fifty Years.*
23. Hardy, Florence Emily, op. cit., p.240.
24. Ibid, p.246.
25. Blathwayt, Raymond, '*A Chat with the* Author of *Tess*', *Black and White*, 27 August 1892.
26. Hardy, Florence Emily, op. cit., Ibid, p.248.
27. Lea, Hermann, *Thomas Hardy's Wessex.*
28. Millgate, Michael and Richard Little Purdy, op. cit., Volume 2, Thomas Hardy to Florence Henniker, 17 August 1893.

3. *Jude the Obscure:* Alterations And Extensions To Max Gate

1. Hardy, Thomas, *Jude the Obscure*, Preface.
2. Ibid, Preface.
3. Ibid, Postscript, April 1912.
4. Hardy, Thomas, *Jude the Obscure*, Chapter VI.
5. The genetic reasons why this is so are now far better understood than was the case in Hardy's day.
6. Millgate, Michael and Richard Little Purdy (editors), *The Collected Letters of Thomas Hardy*, Volume 2, Thomas Hardy to Edmund Gosse, 20 November 1895.
7. *New Review*, June 1894, p.681, in Michael Millgate, *Thomas Hardy: A Biography*, p.357.
8. Emma Hardy to Rebekah Owen, 24 April 1899, Colby College, Waterville, Maine, USA.
9. Hardy, Florence Emily, *The Life of Thomas Hardy*, p.269
10. Millgate, Michael and Richard Little Purdy, op. cit., Volume 2, Thomas Hardy to Florence Henniker, 11 September 1895.
11. Hardy, Florence Emily, op. cit., p.298.
12. Cox, J. Stevens, (general editor): *Monographs on the Life of Thomas Hardy*, Monograph 14, 'Hardyana: A Collection of Short Memorabilia and other Matters of Hardy Interest', 1967, 'The Social Hardy' by Emily Mary Benita Weber.
13. Mrs Patrick Campbell to Mrs S. Coleridge, 12 January 1896, Dorset County Museum.
14. Cox, J. Stevens, (general editor), op. cit., Monograph 14, 'Hardyana: A Collection of Short Memorabilia and other Matters of Hardy Interest', 1967, 'The Social

Hardy' by Emily Mary Benita Weber.
15. Millgate, Michael and Richard Little Purdy (editors), *The Collected Letters of Thomas Hardy*, Volume 2, Thomas Hardy to William Archer, 2 January 1896.
16. Ibid, Volume 2, Thomas Hardy to Emma Lavinia Hardy, 3 February 1896.
17. Ibid, Volume 2, Thomas Hardy to Richard Le Gallienne, 29 June 1896.
18. Ibid, Volume 2, Thomas Hardy to Katharine Hardy, 29 June 1896.
19. Hardy, Florence Emily, op. cit., pp. 284-5.
20. Gifford, Gordon letter to *The Times Literary Supplement*, 1 January 1944.

4. Hardy Reveals Himself Through His Writing

1. Hardy, Thomas, *The Well-Beloved*, Part 1, Chapter 2.
2. Hardy, Evelyn and E. B. Pinion, *One Rare Fair Woman: Thomas Hardy's Letters to Florence Henniker, 1893-1922*, p.xxvi. Hardy's biographer, Evelyn Hardy, has pointed out that although Florence Henniker kept a substantial number of the letters which Hardy wrote to her, many (which may have shed more light on the subject) appear to be missing, the reason being that she 'probably burnt some of them'.
3. Millgate, Michael and Richard Little Purdy (editors), *The Collected Letters of Thomas Hardy*, Volume 2, Thomas Hardy to Florence Henniker, 24 January 1897.
4. Ibid, Volume 2, Thomas Hardy to Thackeray Turner, 28 September 1897.
5. Ibid, Volume 2, Thomas Hardy to Winifred Thomson, 31 October 1897.
6. Ibid, Volume 2, Thomas Hardy to Sir George Douglas, 3 March 1898.
7. Ibid, Volume 2, Thomas Hardy to Elspeth Thomson, 22 February 1898.
8. Ibid, Volume 2, Thomas Hardy to Edmund Gosse, 2 April 1898.
9. Ibid, Volume 2, Thomas Hardy to Katharine Hardy, 26 May 1898.
10. Hardy, Florence Emily, *The Life of Thomas Hardy*, p.54.
11. Millgate, Michael and Richard Little Purdy, op. cit., Volume 2, Thomas Hardy to Katharine Hardy, 11 June 1899.
12. Ibid, Volume 2, Thomas Hardy to Florence Henniker, 25 July 1899.

5. A New Century

1. Millgate, Michael and Richard Little Purdy (editors), *The Collected Letters of Thomas Hardy*, Volume 2, Thomas Hardy to Florence Henniker, 25 February 1900.
2. Ibid, Volume 2, Thomas Hardy to Earl Hodgson, 17 July 1900.
3. Phelps, William Lyon, *Autobiography with Letters*, p.391.
4. Millgate, Michael and Richard Little Purdy, op. cit., Volume 2, Thomas Hardy to Florence Henniker, 22 October 1900.

6. Life Goes On: *The Dynasts* Takes Shape: *Time's Laughingstocks.*

1. Hardy, Florence Emily, *The Life of Thomas Hardy*, pp.310-1.
2. Archer, William, *Real Conversations.*
3. Millgate, Michael and Richard Little Purdy (editors), *The Collected Letters of Thomas Hardy*, Volume 3, Thomas Hardy to Edward Clodd, 2 June 1902.
4. Ibid, Volume 3, Thomas Hardy to Florence Henniker, 25 September 1902.
5. Ibid, Volume 3, Thomas Hardy to Frederic Harrison, 2 January 1903.
6. Ibid, Volume 3, Thomas Hardy to Florence Henniker, 13 September 1903.
7. Gibson, James (editor), *Thomas Hardy: Interviews & Recollections*, p.61.
8. Millgate, Michael and Richard Little Purdy, op. cit., Volume 3, Thomas Hardy to the Reverend Arthur Moule, 20 March 1904.
9. Ibid, Volume 3, Thomas Hardy to Edward Clodd, 12 April 1904.
10. Ibid, Volume 3, Thomas Hardy to Alfred Pope, 11 July 1904.
11. Hardy, Florence Emily, op. cit., p.327.
12. Nevinson, Henry Woodd, *More Changes, More Chances*, pp.179-81.
13. Millgate, Michael and Richard Little Purdy, op. cit., Volume 3, Thomas Hardy to Millicent Fawcett, 30 November 1906.
14. Ibid, Volume 3, Thomas Hardy to Florence Dugdale, 21 March 1907.
15. Cox, J. Stevens, (general editor): *Monographs on the Life of Thomas Hardy*, Monograph 53, 'Hardyana II: A Further Collection of Short Memorabilia and Other Matters of Hardy Interest', 1969, 'Marriage of Thomas Hardy and Florence Dugdale', *Enfield Gazette & Observer*, 13 February 1914.
16. Millgate, Michael and Richard Little Purdy, *The Collected Letters of Thomas Hardy*, Volume 3, Thomas Hardy to Florence Dugdale, 10 August 1905.
17. Hardy, Florence Emily, op. cit., p.334.
18. Hardy, Thomas, *The Dynasts*, Preface.
19. Ibid, Act 7, Scene 8.
20. Ibid, Volume 2, After-Scene.
21. Ibid, Act 1, Scene 5.
22. Millgate, Michael and Richard Little Purdy, op. cit., Volume 3, Thomas Hardy to Lady Grove, 8 August 1908.
23. Ibid, Volume 3, Thomas Hardy to Clive Holland, 5 November 1905. CL
24. Ibid, Volume 4, Thomas Hardy to Henry Newbolt, 16 January 1909.
25. Ibid, Volume 4, Thomas Hardy to the Stinsford Church Restoration Committeee, 25 April 1909.
26. Ibid, Volume 4, Thomas Hardy to Clement Shorter, Early May 1909.
27. Ibid, Volume 4, Thomas Hardy to Florence Henniker, 28 November 1909.

7. From Emma's Standpoint

1. It was only after Emma's death that Hardy discovered *Some Recollections*, which he proceeded to edit and have published.

2. Hardy, Emma, *Some Recollections*, pp.1-2.
3. Ibid, p.6.
4. Millgate, Michael, *Thomas Hardy: A Biography Revisited*, p.326. Clodd, Edward, *Diary* (unpublished), 1 October 1895
5. Clodd, Edward, Diary, 1 October 1895 (Alan Clodd); D. MacCarthy, Hoffman Interview, Hoffman Papers, Miami University of Ohio.
6. Millgate, Michael (editor), *Letters of Emma and Florence Hardy*, Emma L. Hardy to Mary Haweis, 13 Novemmber 1894.
7. Ibid, Emma Hardy to Mary Hardy, 22 February 1896.
8. Ibid, Emma Hardy to Rebekah Owen, 26 December 1906.
9. Gifford, Henry, *Thomas Hardy and Emma*, p.115.
10. Millgate, Michael (editor), op. cit., Emma Hardy to Rebekah Owen, 19 February 1897.
11. Ibid, Emma Hardy to Rebekah Owen, 19 February 1897.
12. Ibid, Emma Hardy to Louise MacCarthy, 3 November 1902.
13. Ibid, Emma Hardy to Lady Hoare, 24 April 1910.
14. Hardy, Emma, op. cit., pp.12,37.
15. Millgate, Michael (editor), op. cit., Emma Hardy to Leonora Gifford, 18 October 1911.

8. What Others Thought Of Emma: A Provisional Diagnosis Of Her Condition

1. Mabel Robinson to I. Cooper Willis, 17 December 1937, Dorset County Museum.
2. Cox, J. Stevens, (general editor): *Monographs on the Life of Thomas Hardy,* Monograph 18, 'Thomas Hardy and his Two Wives' by C.W. Homer, 1964.
3. Millgate, Michael, *Thomas Hardy*, p.479, Professor C.H. Gifford, interview, 1975.
4. Cox, J. Stevens, op. cit., Monograph 14, 'Hardyana: A Collection of Short Memorabilia and other Matters of Hardy Interest', 1967, 'Random Memories of Hardy and Dorset Folk' by Mrs Lorna Stephanie Heenan.
5. Dr F. B. Fisher to Lady Hoare, 25 January 1928, Wiltshire Record Office.
6. Cox, J. Stevens, op. cit., Monograph 16, 'The Homes of Thomas Hardy' by E. L. Evans, 1968.
7. Thwaite, Ann (editor), *Portraits from Life by Edmund Gosse* (Aldershot, Schoar Press, 1991)
8. Flower, Sir Newman, *Just as it Happened*, p.95.
9. Benson, A. C. *Diary*, 5 September 1912, Magdalene College, Cambridge.
10. Hardy, Evelyn and E. B. Pinion, *One Rare Fair Woman: Thomas Hardy's Letters to Florence Henniker, 1893-1922*, p.155.
11. Kay-Robinson, Denys, *The First Mrs Thomas Hardy*, p.235. Edward Clodd, *Diary*, 25 April 1913.
12. Ibid, p.60, Edward Clodd, *Diary*, 27 April 1913.
13. Ibid, p.257, Edward Clodd, *Diary*, 25 April 1913.
14. Millgate, Michael and Richard Little Purdy (editors), *The Collected Letters of*

Thomas Hardy, Volume 5, Thomas Hardy to Florence Henniker, 6 March 1914.
15. Thomas Hardy to Kate Gifford, 23 November 1914, by kind permission of Bristol University Library.
16. Kate Gifford to Thomas Hardy, 25 November 1914, Dorset County Museum.
17. American Psychiatric Association, DSM-IV-TR, p.694.
18. Ibid, p.714.
19. Ibid, p.717.
20. Ibid, p.697.
21. Ibid., p.701.
22. www.bullyonline.org, 19.07.03.
23. Oxford Dictionaries Online.
24. American Psychiatric Association, op. cit., p.325.

9. Hardy, Edward Clodd, And Florence Dugdale

1. Hardy, Florence Emily, *The Life of Thomas Hardy*, p.350.
2. Millgate, Michael and Richard Little Purdy (editors), *The Collected Letters of Thomas Hardy*, Volume 4, Thomas Hardy to Emma Lavinia Hardy, 18 July 1910.
3. Ibid, Volume 4, Thomas Hardy to Lady Gregory, 7 June 1910.

10. Further Insights: Awards: The Death Of Emma

1. Rickett, Arthur Compton, *I Look Back: Memories of Fifty Years.*
2. Millgate, Michael and Richard Little Purdy (editors), *The Collected Letters of Thomas Hardy*, Volume 4, Thomas Hardy to Lady Grove, 13 May 1910.
3. Ibid, Volume 4, Thomas Hardy to Sidney Trist, 18 May 1910.
4. Order of Merit, an order of chivalry founded in 1902 by King Edward VII and limited in number to 24 at any one time within the British Isles.
5. Hardy, Florence Emily, *The Life of Thomas Hardy*, p.350.
6. Millgate, Michael and Richard Little Purdy, op. cit., Volume 4, Thomas Hardy to Emma Lavinia Hardy, 15 July 1910.
7. Ibid, Volume 4, Thomas Hardy to Moberly Bell, 22 July 1910.
8. Ibid, Volume 4, Thomas Hardy to the Superintendent of Dorchester Police, 9 August 1910.
9. Ibid, Volume 4, Thomas Hardy to Florence Henniker, 19 December 1910.
10. Harvey, Alice ('Dolly', née Gale): 'I was Emma Lavinia's Personal Maid', *Thomas Hardy Year Book*, 4 (1974), and interview with Michael Millgate, 1973.
11. Goldring, Douglas, *South Lodge: Reminiscences of Violet Hunt, Ford Madox Ford and the English Review Circle.*
12. Cox, J. Stevens, (general editor): *Monographs on the Life of Thomas Hardy*, Monograph 7, 'Motoring with Thomas Hardy' by Harold Lionel Voss, 1963.
13. Newbolt, Margaret (editor), *The Life and Letters of Sir Henry Newbolt*, pp.166-7.

14. Harvey, Alice ('Dolly', née Gale), op. cit.
15. Flower, Sir Newman, *Just as it Happened*, p.96.
16. Weber, Carl J., *Hardy and the Lady from Madison Square*, p.165.
17. Ibid.
18. Harvey, Alice ('Dolly', née Gale), op. cit.

11. An Outpouring Of Poetry

1. Gifford, Henry, *Thomas Hardy and Emma*, p.116.
2. Cox, J. Stevens, (general editor): *Monographs on the Life of Thomas Hardy*, Monograph 65, 'Cook at Max Gate 1913-1914' by Annie Mitchell, 1970.
3. Millgate, Michael and Richard Little Purdy (editors), *The Collected Letters of Thomas Hardy*, Volume 4, Thomas Hardy to the Reverend J. H. Dickinson, 16 February 1914.
4. Ibid, Volume 5, Thomas Hardy to Frederic Harrison, 17 February 1914.
5. Ibid, Volume 5, Thomas Hardy to Reymond Abbott, 10 May 1914.
6. Cox, J. Stevens, op. cit., Monograph 7, 'Motoring with Thomas Hardy' by Harold Lionel Voss, 1963.
7. Ibid, Monograph 20, 'Thomas Hardy through the Camera's Eye' by Hermann Lea, 1964.
8. Millgate, Michael and Richard Little Purdy, op. cit., Volume 5, Thomas Hardy to Edward Clodd, 18 August 1914?
9. Gifford, Henry, op. cit., pp.120-1.
10. Millgate, Michael and Richard Little Purdy, op. cit., Volume 5, Thomas Hardy to Florence Henniker, 23 December 1914.
11. Ibid, Volume 5, Thomas Hardy to Hamo Thornycroft, 14 April 1915.
12. Ibid, Volume 5, Thomas Hardy to Sydney Cockerell, 5 December 1915.
13. Cox, J. Stevens, op. cit., Monograph 61, 'Hardy as I Knew Him' by E. J. Stevens, 1969.
14. Millgate, Michael and Richard Little Purdy, op. cit., Volume 5, Thomas Hardy to Sydney Cockerell, 23 February 1917.
15. Hardy, Florence Emily, *The Life of Thomas Hardy*, pp.375-6.
16. Millgate, Michael and Richard Little Purdy, op. cit., Volume 5, Thomas Hardy to Lewis Chase, 15 May 1917.

12. Onwards, Towards Eighty Years Of Age

1. Hardy, Florence Emily, *The Life of Thomas Hardy*, p.384.
2. Millgate, Michael (editor), *Letters of Emma and Florence Hardy*, Florence Hardy to Sydney Cockerell, 17 February l918.
3. Cox, J. Stevens, (general editor): *Monographs on the Life of Thomas Hardy*, Monograph 15, 'Thomas Hardy as a Musician' by J. V. Mardon, 1964.

4. Ibid.
5. Ibid.
6. Hardy, Florence Emily, op. cit., p.387.
7. Millgate, Michael and Richard Little Purdy, *The Collected Letters of Thomas Hardy*, Volume 5, Thomas Hardy to Sir George Douglas, 7 May 1910.
8. Hardy, Florence Emily, op. cit., p.390.
9. Millgate, Michael and Richard Little Purdy, op. cit., Volume 5, Thomas Hardy to Florence Henniker, 5 June 1919.
10. Cox, J. Stevens, op. cit., Monograph 14, 'Hardyana: A Collection of Short Memorabilia and other Matters of Hardy Interest', 1967, 'Glimpses of Thomas Hardy' by Robert Harding.
11. Felkin, Elliott, 'Days with Thomas Hardy', *Encounter*, April 1962.
12. Millgate, Michael (editor), op. cit., Florence Hardy to Louise Yearsley, 10 August 1919.
13. Ibid, Florence Hardy to Sydney Cockerell, 19 August 1919.
14. Ibid, Florence Hardy to Sydney Cockerell, 25 Sep 1919.
15. Thomas Hardy to Charles Edwin Gifford, 3 November 1919, Bristol University Library: Special Collections.
16. Millgate, Michael (editor), op. cit., Florence Hardy to Sydney Cockerell, 27 December 1919.
17. Graves, Robert, the *Sphere,* 28 January 1928, p.129.
18. Millgate, Michael and Richard Little Purdy, op. cit., Volume 6, Thomas Hardy to Harold Child, 4 May 1920.
19. Cox, J. Stevens, op. cit., Monograph 14, 'Hardyana: A Collection of Short Memorabilia and other Matters of Hardy Interest', 1967, 'Cleaner at Max Gate' by Mrs Margaret Male.
20. Hardy, Florence Emily, op. cit., p.405.
21. Graves, Robert, *Goodbye to All That*, pp.248-9, 251.
22. Graves, Robert, the *Sphere*, pp.135-6.
23. Hardy, Florence Emily, op. cit., p.407.
24. Millgate, Michael and Richard Little Purdy, op. cit., Volume 6, Thomas Hardy to an unidentified correspondent, December 1920.
25. Millgate, Michael (editor), op. cit., Florence Hardy to Sydney Cockerell, 26 December 1920. Gertrude Bugler married her cousin, Ernest H. Bugler, farmer of Woodbury House, Beaminster, Dorsetshire.
26. Ibid, Florence Hardy to Louise Yearsley, 30 December 1920.
27. Ibid, Florence Hardy to Howard Bliss, 3 April 1921.
28. Asquith, Lady Cynthia, 'Thomas Hardy at Max Gate', *The Listener*, 7 June 1956.
29. Ervine, St John, 'Hardy and his Friends', BBC Radio, 19 February 1955.
30. Masefield, John, *So Long to Learn*, p.221

13. ***Late Lyrics and Earlier***

1. Hardy, Florence Emily, *The Life of Thomas Hardy*, p.415.
2. Cox, J. Stevens, (general editor), op. cit., Monograph 4, 'Miss E. E. T. (Hardy's Parlour-Maid), The Domestic Life of Thomas Hardy (1921-1928)', 1963.
3. Ibid, Monograph 4, 'The Domestic Life of Thomas Hardy' by Ellen E. Titterington, 1963.
4. Ibid, Monograph 7, 'Motoring with Thomas Hardy' by H. L. Voss, 1963.
5. Ibid, Monograph 6, 'Thomas Hardy in his Garden' by Bertie Norman Stephens, 1963.
6. Ibid, Monograph 14, 'Hardyana: A Collection of Short Memorabilia and other Matters of Hardy Interest', 1967, 'Cleaner at Max Gate' by Mrs Margaret Male.

14. Final Years

1. Hart-Davis, Rupert (editor), *Siegfried Sassoon, Diaries 1920-1922.*
2. Millgate, Michael (editor), *Letters of Emma and Florence Hardy*, Florence Hardy to Sydney Cockerell, 3 August 1922.
3. Millgate, Michael and Richard Little Purdy (editors), *The Collected Letters of Thomas Hardy*, Volume 6, Thomas Hardy to Lady Sackville, 25 November 1922.
4. Cox, J. Stevens, (general editor): *Monographs on the Life of Thomas Hardy*, Monograph 8, 'Thomas Hardy: His Secretary Remembers' by May O'Rourke, 1965.
5. Ibid, Monograph 53, 'Hardyana II: A Further Collection of Short Memorabilia and Other Matters of Hardy Interest', 1969, 'He Worked at Max Gate', William Weston to James Stevens Cox, 26 July 1968.
6. Ibid, Monograph 4, 'Miss E. E. T. (Hardy's Parlour-Maid), The Domestic Life of Thomas Hardy (1921-1928)', 1963.
7. Millgate, Michael and Richard Little Purdy, op. cit., Thomas Hardy to Clive Holland, 25 August 1923.
8. Millgate, Michael (editor), op. cit., Florence Hardy to Marie Stopes, 14 September 1923.
9. Cox, J. Stevens, op. cit., Monograph 6, 'Thomas Hardy in his Garden' by Bertie Norman Stephens, 1963.
10. Hardy, Kate, *Diaries.*
11. Millgate, Michael and Richard Little Purdy, op. cit., Volume 6, Thomas Hardy to J. H. Morgan, 21 April 1924.
12. Woodhall, Augusta Noreen, *Norrie's Tale: An Autobiography of the last of the Hardy Players*, pp.31-2.
13. Atkins, Norman J., *Thomas Hardy and the Hardy Players.*
14. Gibson, James (editor), *Thomas Hardy: Interviews & Recollections*, p.211
15. Norman, Andrew, *Thomas Hardy: Bockhampton and Beyond.*
16. Atkins, Norman J., op. cit.
17. Hardy, Kate, *Diaries.*

18. Atkins, Norman J., op. cit.
19. Ibid.
20. Woodhall, Augusta Noreen, op. cit, p.34.
21. Cox, J. Stevens, op. cit., Monograph 4, 'Afterthoughts of Max Gate', by Ellen E. Titterington, 1969.
22. Ibid, Monograph 15, 'Thomas Hardy as a Musician by J. Vera Mardon', 1964.
23. Hardy, Kate, *Diaries*.
24. Cox, J. Stevens, op. cit., Monograph 7, 'Motoring with Thomas Hardy' by Harold Lionel Voss, 1963.
25. Ibid, Monograph 14, 'Hardyana: A Collection of Short Memorabilia and other Matters of Hardy Interest', 1967, 'Hardy Honoured by Bristol University', by Dr Thomas Loveday,
26. Millgate, Michael (editor), op. cit., Florence Hardy to Sydney Cockerell, 8 August 1925.
27. Cox, J. Stevens, op. cit., Monograph 4, 'Miss E. E. T. (Hardy's Parlour-Maid), The Domestic Life of Thomas Hardy (1921-1928)', 1963.
28. Smith, Major General Sir Henry Marriott, 'Hardy and his Friends', BBC Radio, 19 February 1955.
29. Seymour-Smith, Martin, *Hardy*, p.38.
30. Hardy, Kate, *Diaries*.
31. Cox, J. Stevens, op. cit., Monograph 4, 'Miss E. E. T. (Hardy's Parlour-Maid), The Domestic Life of Thomas Hardy (1921-1928)', 1963.
32. Hardy, Florence Emily, *The Life of Thomas Hardy*, p.430.
33. Millgate, Michael (editor), op. cit., Florence Hardy to Sydney Cockerell, Christmas Day 1925.
34. Hardy, Florence Emily, op. cit., p.431.
35. Millgate, Michael and Richard Little Purdy, op. cit., Volume 7, Thomas Hardy to Revd H. G. B. Cowley, 27 February 1926.
36. Millgate, Michael (editor), op. cit., Florence Hardy to Philip Ridgeway, 16 March 1926.
37. Millgate, Michael and Richard Little Purdy, op. cit., Volume 7, Thomas Hardy to Edward Clodd, 1 July 1926.
38. Cox, J. Stevens, op. cit., Monograph 4, 'Afterthoughts of Max Gate', by Ellen E. Titterington, 1969.
39. Ibid, Monograph 6, 'Thomas Hardy in his Garden' by Bertie Norman Stephens, 1963.
40. Ibid, Monograph 4, 'Miss E. E. T. (Hardy's Parlour-Maid), The Domestic Life of Thomas Hardy (1921-1928)', 1963.
41. Hardy, Florence Emily, *The Life of Thomas Hardy*, p.439.
42. Squire, J.C., *Sunday Mornings*, pp.289-300.
43. Glasgow, Ellen, *The Woman Within.*
44. Cox, J. Stevens, op. cit., Monograph 7, 'Motoring with Thomas Hardy' by Harold Lionel Voss, 1963.
45. Gibson, James (editor), *Thomas Hardy: Interviews & Recollections*, p.62

46. Hardy, Florence Emily op. cit., p.443.
47. Millgate, Michael and Richard Little Purdy, op. cit., Volume 7, Thomas Hardy to Sir Edmund Gosse, Xmas Day 1927.
48. Mann, Dr. Edward W., BBC Radio, 1955.
49. Hardy, Florence Emily, *The Life of Thomas Hardy*, p.445.
50. Mann, Dr. Edward W., BBC Radio, 1955.
51. Cox, J. Stevens, op. cit., Monograph 4, 'Miss E. E. T. (Hardy's Parlour-Maid), The Domestic Life of Thomas Hardy (1921-1928)', 1963.

15. Aftermath

1. Mann, Dr. Edward W., BBC Radio, 1955.
2. Hardy, Kate, *Diaries*.
3. Cox, J. Stevens, (general editor): *Monographs on the Life of Thomas Hardy*, Monograph 12, 'Memories of Mr. & Mrs. Thomas Hardy', by D. M. Meech, 1963.
4. Hardy, Florence Emily, *The Life of Thomas Hardy*, p.53.
5. Hardy, Kate, *Diaries*.
6. Ibid.
7. Atkins, Norman J., *Thomas Hardy and the Hardy Players*.
8. Cox, J. Stevens, op. cit., Monograph 4, 'Miss E. E. T. (Hardy's Parlour-Maid), The Domestic Life of Thomas Hardy (1921-1928)', 1963.
9. Ibid, Monograph 6, 'Thomas Hardy in his Garden' by Bertie Norman Stephens, 1963.
10. Hardy, Kate, *Diaries*.
11. Cox, J. Stevens, op. cit., Monograph 6, 'Thomas Hardy in his Garden' by Bertie Norman Stephens, 1963.
12. Taylor, Richard H. (editor), *The Personal Notebooks of Thomas Hardy*, p.100-1.
13. Cox, J. Stevens, op. cit., Monograph 36, 'Thomas Hardy's Will and Other Wills of His Family', 1967.
14. Ibid, Monograph 4, 'Miss E. E. T. (Hardy's Parlour-Maid), The Domestic Life of Thomas Hardy (1921-1928)', 1963.
15. Millgate, Michael (editor), *Letters of Emma and Florence Hardy*, Florence Hardy to Edmund Gosse, 5 February 1918.
16. Ibid, Florence Hardy to T. E. Lawrence, 5 March 1928.
17. Cox, J. Stevens, op. cit., Monograph 6, 'Thomas Hardy in his Garden' by Bertie Norman Stephens, 1963.
18. Hardy, Kate, *Diaries*.
19. Ibid.
20. Ibid.
21. Cox, J. Stevens, op. cit., Monograph 36, 'Thomas Hardy's Will and Other Wills of His Family', 1967.
22. Millgate, Michael (editor), op. cit., Florence Hardy to Siegfried Sassoon, 11 July 1929.

23. Woodhall, Augusta Noreen, *Norrie's Tale: An Autobiography of the last of the Hardy Players*, p.34.
24. Hardy, Kate, *Diaries*.
25. Ibid.
26. Millgate, Michael (editor), op. cit., Florence Hardy to Howard Bliss, 29 September 1929.
27. Hardy, Kate, *Diaries*.
28. Ibid.
29. Millgate, Michael (editor), op. cit., Florence Hardy to Howard Bliss, 10 January 1931.
30. Hardy, Kate, *Diaries*.
31. Ibid.
32. Phelps, William Lyon, *Autobiography with Letters*, pp 396-7
33. Hardy, Kate, *Diaries*.
34. Ibid.
35. Ibid.
36. Ibid.
37. Millgate, Michael (editor), op. cit., p.347.
38. Ibid, p.349.
39. Ibid, Florence Hardy to Christine Wood Homer, 11 May 1937.
40. Cox, J. Stevens, op. cit., Monograph 36, 'Thomas Hardy's Will and Other Wills of His Family', 1967.
41. Hardy, Kate, *Diaries*.
42. Cox, J. Stevens, op. cit., Monograph 36, 'Thomas Hardy's Will and Other Wills of His Family', 1967.

BIBLIOGRAPHY

American Psychiatric Association. *Diagnostic and Statistical Manual of Mental Disorders (DSM-IV-TR)* (American Psychiatric Association, Washington, DC, 2000)

Andrews, Charles T., *The Dark Awakening: A History of St Lawrence's Hospital* (Cox & Wyman, London, 1978)

Archer, William, *Real Conversations* (W. Heinemann, London 1904)

Atkins, Norman J., *Thomas Hardy and the Hardy Players* (Toucan Press, Guernsey, 1980)

Benson, A.C., *Diary* (Magdalene College, Cambridge, 5 September 1912)

Blunden, Edmund, *Thomas Hardy* (Macmillan, London, 1967)

Chesterton, G. K., *Autobiography* (Sheed & Ward, London, 1936)

Collins, Vere H., *Talks with Thomas Hardy at Max Gate* (Gerald Duckworth, London, 1978)

Comer, Ronald J., *Fundamentals of Abnormal Psychology* (2nd edition) (Worth Publishers, Inc., New York, 1999)

Cox, J. Stevens, (general editor): *Monographs on the Life of Thomas Hardy*, Nos 1-72, (Toucan Press, Beaminster, Dorset and Guernsey)

Dictionary of National Biography (Oxford University Press)

Egerton, George, *Keynotes* (Garland Publishing Inc., New York & London, reprint of the 1893 edition published by Roberts Bros, Boston, USA)

Flower, Sir Newman, *Just as it Happened* (Cassell & Company, London, 1950)

Gelder, Michael, Paul Harrison and Philip Cowen, *Shorter Oxford Textbook of Psychiatry* (Oxford University Press, 2006)

Gibson, James (editor), *Thomas Hardy: Interviews & Recollections* (Macmillan, London, 1999)

Gifford, Henry, 'Thomas Hardy and Emma', in *Essays and Studies* (edited by R.M. Wilson) (John Murray, London, 1966)

Gittings, Robert, *Young Thomas Hardy* (Penguin Books, London, 1975)

Glasgow, Ellen, *The Woman Within* (Hill & Wang, New York, 1954)

Goldring, Douglas, *South Lodge: Reminiscences of Violet Hunt, Ford Madox Ford and the English Review Circle*, (Constable, London, 1943)

Graves, Robert *Goodbye to All That* (Jonathan Cape, London 1929)

Gregory, Richard L. (editor), *The Oxford Companion to the Mind* (Oxford University Press, 1987)

Hamlin, Garland, *Afternoon Neighbours* (New York, 1934)

Hands, Timothy, *Thomas Hardy and Stinsford Church* (Stinsford Parochial

Church Council)
Hardy, Emma, *Diaries* (edited by Richard H. Taylor) (Carcanet New Press and Mid-Northumberland Arts Group
Manchester, 1985)
Hardy, Emma, *Some Recollections* (Oxford University Press, 1979)
Hardy, Evelyn and F. B. Pinion, *One Rare Fair Woman: Thomas Hardy's Letters to Florence Henniker, 1893-1922* (Macmillan, London, 1972)
Hardy, Evelyn, *Thomas Hardy: A Critical Biography* (The Hogarth Press, London, 1954)
Hardy, Florence Emily, *The Life of Thomas Hardy* (Macmillan Publishers, London, 1965)
Hardy, Katharine ('Kate'), *Diary* no 1: 1 January 1915 - 31 August 1918; *Diary* no 2: September 1918 - 31 May 1928; *Diary* no 3: 2 June 1928 - 30 November 1939. The Lock Collection, courtesy Dorset County Museum.
Hardy, Thomas, *The Complete Poems* (edited by James Gibson) (Macmillan, London, 1976)
Hardy, Thomas, 'The New Wessex Edition' of his novels, including *Desperate Remedies, Far from the Madding Crowd, The Hand of Ethelberta, Jude the Obscure, A Laodicean, The Mayor of Casterbridge, A Pair of Blue Eyes, The Return of the Native, Tess of the D'Urbervilles, The Trumpet-Major, Two on a Tower, Under the Greenwood Tree, The Well-Beloved*, and *The Woodlanders*. (Macmillan, London, 1990)
Hardy, Thomas, *Notebook* (edited with notes by Evelyn Hardy) (Hogarth Press, London, 1955)
Hardy, Thomas, *The Personal Notebooks of Thomas Hardy* (edited by Richard H. Taylor) (Macmillan, London, 1978)
Hart-Davis, Rupert (editor), *Siegfried Sassoon, Diaries 1920-1922* (Faber, London, 1981)
Hawkins, Desmond, *Hardy, Novelist and Poet* (David & Charles, London, 1976)
Helier, Lady St, *Memories of Fifty Years* (Edward Arnold, 1909)
Kay-Robinson, Denys, *The First Mrs Thomas Hardy* (Macmillan, London, 1979)
Kay-Robinson, Denys, 'The Face at the Casement', *Thomas Hardy Year Book*, No. 5, pp.34-5.
Lago, Mary, and P. N. Furbank, *Selected Letters of E. M. Forster*, London, Collins, 1983-1985)
Lasselin, Georges, *Le Couple Humain dans l'Oeuvre de Thomas Hardy* (Busson, Paris, 1928)
Lea, Hermann, *Thomas Hardy's Wessex* (Macmillan, London, 1913)
Leah, Andrew H., 'Mr Hardy's Escape Route' (The National Trust)

Leah, Andrew H., 'The Max Gate Waterworks' (The National Trust)
Leah, Andrew H., 'The Pet's Cemetery' (The National Trust)
Leah, Andrew H., 'What Lies Beneath? The Archaeology of Max Gate' (The National Trust)
Lewer, David, *Hardy in Swanage* (Dorset Publishing Company, Wincanton, 1990)
Lewis, Heulyn and & Ginny Lewis, *In the Footsteps of Thomas and Emma Hardy* (North Cornwall Coast and Countryside Service, 2003)
MacCarthy, Desmond, *Memories* (MacGibbon & Kee, London, 1953)
Masefield, John, *So Long to Learn* (Heinemann, London 1952)
Millgate, Michael and Richard Little Purdy (editors), *Collected Letters of Thomas Hardy*, Volumes 1-7 (Clarendon Press, Oxford, 1996)
Millgate, Michael (editor), *Letters of Emma and Florence Hardy* (Clarendon Press, Oxford, 1996)
Millgate, Michael, *Thomas Hardy: A Biography* (Oxford University Press, 1982)
Millgate, Michael *Thomas Hardy: A Biography Revisited* (Oxford University Press, 2006)
Milne, James, *The Memoirs of a Bookman* (John Murray, London 1934)
Murry, John Middleton, *Katherine Mansfield and Other Literary Portraits* (Peter Nevill, London 1949)
Nevinson, Henry Woodd, *More Changes, More Chances* (Nisbet & Co., London, 1925)
Newbolt, Margaret (editor), *The Life and Letters of Sir Henry Newbolt* (Faber & Faber, London, 1942)
Norman, Andrew, *Thomas Hardy: Bockhampton and Beyond* (Fonthill, Stroud, 2016)
Phelps, Kenneth, *Annotations by Thomas Hardy in his Bibles and Prayer Book* in *Thomas Hardy: Materials for a Study of his Life, Times and Works* (edited by J. Stevens Cox), Monograph No. 32.
Phelps, Kenneth, *The Wormwood Cup* (Lodenek Press, Cornwall, 1975)
Phelps, William Lyon, *Autobiography with Letters* (Oxford University Press, 1939)
Phillpotts, Eden, *From the Angle of 88* (Hutchinson, London 1951)
Pitfield, F.R., *Hardy's Wessex Locations* (Halsgrove, Tiverton, 1992)
Pryor, Eric H., *Claybury 1893-1993: A Century of Caring* (Mental Health Care Group and Forest Health Care Trust, 1993)
Purdy, Richard Little, *Thomas Hardy: A Bibliographical Study* (Clarendon Press, Oxford, 1954)
Rickett, Arthur Compton, *I Look Back: Memories of Fifty Years* (Jenkins, London, 1933)

Sassoon Siegfried, *I Look Back: Memories of Fifty Years* (Jenkins, London, 1933)
Sassoon, Siegfried, *The Old Huntsman and Other Poems* (Heinemann, London 1917)
Seymour-Smith, Martin, *Hardy* (Bloomsbury, London, 1994)
Squire, J. C., *Sunday Mornings* (Heinemann, London, 1930)
Stewart, J. I. M., *Thomas Hardy: A Critical Biography* (Longman Group, London, 1971)
Story of the Tolpuddle Martyrs, The (Trades Union Congress, London, 1991)
Taylor, Richard H. (editor), *The Personal Notebooks of Thomas Hardy* (Macmillan, London, 1978)
Weber, Carl J., *Hardy and the Lady from Madison Square* (Colby College Press, Maine, USA, 1952) Quotations by kind permission of the publishers)
Wilson, Chris M. and & Andrew J. Oswald, 'How Does Marriage Affect Physical and Psychological Health? A Survey of the Longitudinal Evidence', Discussion Paper No. 1619, Bonn, Germany: IZA
Winchcombe, Anna. *Hardy's Cottage* (The National Trust, London, 1981)
Windle, Bertram C. A. *The Wessex of Thomas Hardy* (John Lane, The Bodley Head, London, 1902)
Woodhall, Augusta Noreen, *Norrie's Tale: An Autobiography of the last of the Hardy Players* (A Lullworde publication, Lulworth Cover, Wareham, Dorset, 2006)
Zachrisson, R. E., *Hardy as Man, Writer and Philosopher* (Stockholm, 1928)

BY THE SAME AUTHOR

By Swords Divided: Corfe Castle in the Civil War. Halsgrove, 2003.
Dunshay: Reflections on a Dorset Manor House. Halsgrove, 2004.
Sir Francis Drake: Behind the Pirate's Mask. Halsgrove, 2004.
Thomas Hardy: Christmas Carollings. Halsgrove, 2005.
Enid Blyton and her Enchantment with Dorset. Halsgrove, 2005.
Agatha Christie: The Finished Portrait. Tempus, 2007.
Tyneham: A Tribute. Halsgrove, 2007.
Mugabe: Teacher, Revolutionary, Tyrant. The History Press, 2008.
T. E. Lawrence: The Enigma Explained. The History Press, 2008.
The Story of George Loveless and the Tolpuddle Martyrs. Halsgrove, 2008.
Father of the Blind: A Portrait of Sir Arthur Pearson. The History Press, 2009.
Agatha Christie: The Finished Portrait. Tempus, 2006.
Agatha Christie: The Pitkin Guide. Pitkin Publishing, 2009.
Jane Austen: An Unrequited Love. The History Press, 2009.
Arthur Conan Doyle: The Man behind Sherlock Holmes. The History Press, 2009.
HMS Hood: Pride of the Royal Navy. The History Press, 2009.
Purbeck Personalities. Halsgrove, 2009.
Bournemouth's Founders and Famous Visitors. The History Press, 2010.
Jane Austen: An Unrequited Love. The History Press, 2009.
Thomas Hardy: Behind the Mask. The History Press, 2011.
Hitler: Dictator or Puppet. Pen & Sword Books, 2011.
A Brummie Boy goes to War. Halsgrove, 2011.
Winston Churchill: Portrait of an Unquiet Mind. Pen & Sword Books, 2012.
Charles Darwin: Destroyer of Myths. Pen & Sword Books, 2013.
Beatrix Potter: Her Inner World. Pen & Sword Books, 2013.
T. E. Lawrence: Tormented Hero. Fonthill, 2014.
Agatha Christie: The Disappearing Novelist. Fonthill, 2014.
Lawrence of Arabia's Clouds Hill. Halsgrove, 2014.
Jane Austen: Love is Like a Rose. Fonthill, 2015.
Kindly Light: The Story of Blind Veterans UK. Fonthill, 2015.

Author's website www.andrew-norman.com

INDEX